— Jona —

Cele[...]
and [...]
ach[...]
God speed on your

TO

Jonathan

FROM with
Love,
Mimi

DATE

31 August 2023

new chapter
in life!
Love you,
Mimi

# WORDS
## OF JESUS
### FOR MEN

CHRISTIAN ART
PUBLISHERS

Originally published by Christelike Uitgewersmaatskappy
under the title *Jesus se woorde vir mans*

© 2015

English edition
© 2015 Christian Art Publishers
PO Box 1599, Vereeniging, 1930, RSA

First edition 2015

Translated by Annegreth Rautenbach

Cover designed by Christian Art Publishers

Images used under license from Shutterstock.com

Set in 12 on 14pt Avenir LT Std
by Christian Art Publishers

Printed in China

ISBN 978-1-4321-2166-2

15  16  17  18  19  20  21  22  23  24  –  12  11  10  9  8  7  6  5  4  3

# FOREWORD

▶ I'm very excited about this book for one simple reason: It's all about the words of Jesus. The things He says are not mere opinions, but life-giving truths that can radically change a person's life.

Peter said the following about this topic: "Lord, to whom shall we go? You have the words of eternal life. We have come to believe and to know that You are the Holy One of God" (John 6:68-69).

May these words and the Author thereof deeply impact your life.

Riekert Botha
Vredendal

# JANUARY

# THE GOLDEN RULE

*"Do to others as you would have them do to you."*
Luke 6:31

This has been a radical statement throughout the ages. We grow up in a world that thinks it is fine to treat other people like they treat us (and at the same time we expect them to treat us differently or better than we treat them).

Jesus tells us God's comments about this. What is wrong is wrong – not only when we are at the receiving end of lovelessness, unfairness or immaturity, but also when we are the distributors. To heed these words of Jesus means to acknowledge Him as righteous Judge of the nations and to understand that He will deal accordingly with injustices – no matter who committed them. There is no justification for being without love – ever.

To embrace these words is to acknowledge Jesus' authority in your life and to discover life itself!

According to Jesus we are unholy and impure if we want to get even with someone. Rather act from God's rich treasury and share in the feast!

# A WINNING SPIRIT

*"What good is it for someone to gain the whole world, and yet lose or forfeit their very self?"*
Luke 9:25

For many of us, winning or losing is our main goal in life. We want to win arguments, win in the marketplace, on the sports fields, in relationships, and we never want to feel like losers.

Jesus warns us that the wrong winning spirit can cost us everything. It's possible to win everything, but lose the greatest thing – yourself.

Don't forfeit your soul for the sake of inferior finishing lines. Win respectably – like Jesus says. Not standing under Jesus' authority is to lose life, even if the world is cheering you on as the winner. Your soul is more precious than anything. Never lose it or throw it away.

Side with Jesus, even if it means losing everything according to the world's standards. In this way you will receive the honor of being recognized and counted with the greatest and most important Winner of all time.

# THE CORRECT INFORMATION

*"Why do you look at the speck of sawdust in your brother's eye and pay no attention to the plank in your own eye?"*
Matthew 7:3

This is a straightforward question! It runs deep into the deceitfulness of my own heart. I can appear to be informed and well read about other people's lives and actions, and be completely blind to my own sinfulness.

Jesus' message is very clear: "Focus on your own heart, and leave the person next to you. It's not worth it to always want to fix other people, but your own heart is unclean before Me. I don't need you to explain others' faults to Me. I know all about them. What bothers Me is that you're not aware of all the things going on in your own life. Allow Me to remove the plank in *your* life, and then we can talk about the pieces of sawdust in the eyes of your children, spouse, mother-in-law, employees and colleagues."

Lord Jesus, I'm quick to judge other people's actions as wrong, unfair or without love, but I hide my own deeds. Please help me to stand before You with a pure heart, regardless of what others are doing. Amen.

# TRUE GENEROSITY

*"When you give to the needy, do not let your left hand know what your right hand is doing, so that your giving may be in secret."*
Matthew 6:3-4

One of the things that stand out for me about Jesus is the absolute purity of His heart. With Him there are no hidden agendas or masked schemes. In stark contrast stands my own life: full of evil.

It is possible for me to perform acts of love with impure motives in my heart. Don't love others and be kind to them for your own selfish reasons. Don't misuse the poor to try and show the world how great you are. If you want to help them, do so without ulterior motives. The Father rewards pureness of heart and obedience, but He hates hypocrisy.

True love is performing good deeds and doing what is right without receiving any recognition or reward.

Lord Jesus, I desire a heart like Yours. Come to the aid of my flesh and reveal Your truth in my life. Amen.

# I'M THE PROOF

*"For God so loved the world that He gave His one and only Son, that whoever believes in Him shall not perish but have eternal life."*
John 3:16

This popular Scripture verse is the actual words of Jesus Christ. Because they come from the mouth of Jesus, they are so much more authoritative.

He says, "Here it is. *I'm* the living proof that the Father loves you very much. *I'm* the indisputable proof that God doesn't neglect you and treat you in a second-hand way. You might not know the Father that well, but I know Him very well.

"I take comfort in being close to Him. You might not know yet what I'm doing here, but I know very well. I'm going to show you true love. I'm going to love you for all eternity. Those who accept this truth will live by it. But those who reject it will never see God."

Father, thank You for sending Jesus to show me how much You love me. Minister to me through this love. Change me through this love. I want to live according to it. Amen.

# THE GREATEST IN THE KINGDOM

*"Anyone who wants to be first must be the very last, and the servant of all."*
Mark 9:35

▶ Jesus' words make me smile. It's so deliberately opposed to everything the world stands for. The disciples were always concerned about who would be the greatest in God's kingdom. We often have this problem too. Who is the most clever, strongest, most important, well read, best, prettiest, most sought after, most successful, richest and most spiritual?

Then Jesus explains: "In the world, the strongest and most overpowering people usually stand out above everyone else, and they want to rule and control everyone. But it doesn't work this way in God's kingdom. It doesn't matter what you've accomplished or how important you may be; what matters is if you can love without being loved in return. This counts the most in God's eyes. For such people God has a special regard. Don't take God's fondness for people too lightly."

Lord, help! It's easy to say that Your words are more important than those of the world, but then my words and deeds reveal something different. Please teach me more of Your character and attitude. Amen.

# CHERISH RELATIONSHIPS

*"If your brother or sister sins, go and point out their fault, just between the two of you. If they listen to you, you have won them over."*
Matthew 18:15

▶ Jesus is the Master of relationships. He wins over hearts and friendships. Jesus says, "Friends, it's not about being offended or cutting someone out. If someone has hurt you, don't just shut your heart against them. Cherish the relationship more than your wounded pride. Go to the person and make an effort to resolve the matter.

"If you've been hurt, tell your friend. If the person stands under My authority, they won't be offended. In this way you can reconcile and save the relationship. And if they don't want to listen to you, try again and again and again, until you see that the case is beyond redemption. But do everything you can to prevent the relationship from ending."

To shut your heart when you get hurt is quick and easy, but God's way is different. Walk in *His* way towards true life!

# LIKE HONEY IN THE MORNING SUN

*"Blessed are the pure in heart, for they will see God."*
Matthew 5:8

The word *pure* literally indicates how honey is purified from all the things one usually finds in raw honey, like little bee wings and feet and other "bee souvenirs." Pure honey is a clean, deep-gold color that shines in the morning sun.

God is a God of the heart. Doing good deeds with an impure heart is repulsive to Him. Jesus specializes in purifying hearts. The more we surrender and expose our inside world to Him to purify, the clearer God becomes to us. Impure hearts battle to see God, but a pure heart can enjoy God's presence.

These words of Jesus are actually an open invitation for us: "Come, friends! Don't wait any longer to share in the feast!"

Lord Jesus, thank You for loving me enough to remove my masks and pretences so that I can experience You. Thank You for the privilege of being purified by You. Amen.

# MINGLE WITH THE RIGHT PEOPLE

*"It is not the healthy who need a doctor, but the sick. I have not come to call the righteous, but sinners."*
Mark 2:17

Jesus was rather unpopular amongst the pretend-believers. They couldn't stand Him. While they were pretending to be so spiritual, Jesus ate with sinners and outcasts. They were very offended by this. How dare He mingle with undesirable people – He who taught people about God!

Jesus' answer was simple: "That's exactly the people God has in mind. They know they are lost and undesirable, and they long for salvation. But those who pretend to be fine (when they are not) miss out on God's salvation. They are so busy showing others how holy they are that they turn down God's offer of true holiness. How silly! God didn't send Me to play false games, but to reconcile the needy with God."

Thank You, Jesus. Thank You so much. You came to earth for me… Help me to follow in Your steps and not of those around me. Amen.

# DO ALL PEOPLE HAVE A PRICE?

*Jesus answered, "It is written: 'Worship the Lord your God and serve Him only.'"*
Luke 4:8

The devil is shrewd and arrogant. He tried to tempt Jesus to sin with artful distortions of the Bible. In this Scripture passage in Luke 4, he makes Jesus an offer if He worships him. He almost makes it sound like a "once-in-a-lifetime deal" – take it or leave it.

The offer included honor, power, status, success and unprecedented prestige in return for loyalty. The simplicity and purity of Jesus' answer is astonishing: "No offer of success and power is enough to shift My loyalty from God. I do not have a price tag. Even if I go to waste in the dust, I will bow My knee before Him alone. He will defend Me and reward Me – even unto death."

You've probably received a similar offer more than once in many hidden forms, and you will probably hear many more. Don't give up your birthright for a bowl of soup!

# HE TRIUMPHS OVER ALL

*"Do not let your hearts be troubled. You believe in God; believe also in Me."*
John 14:1

These words came amid very upsetting news for the disciples: Jesus told them that criminals would take Him captive and kill Him. What! How is that possible – He is the Messiah!

He then told them, "Friends, believe that God is who He says He is. Believe that I am who I say I am. Do not allow sudden evil and bad news to upset you and shake you. We are still who We said We are, no matter what happens. Nothing can change this – not even death.

"Wait and see; you'll experience for yourself firsthand during the next few days. Then you will be absolutely convinced that nothing can separate you from Me – not suffering or trouble or prosecution, hunger or nudity, danger or sword."

Never allow difficult times to overpower the glory and omnipotence of God. He triumphs far above all – even when you go through the darkest valley.

# PRAY THE RIGHT WAY

*"When you stand praying, if you hold anything against anyone, forgive them, so that your Father in heaven may forgive you your sins."*
Mark 11:25

At a previous congregation where I served, the people were strongly encouraged to pray more. Before this, when it seemed like no breakthroughs emerged, the members said, "It's because we don't pray enough." I agreed. It's important to talk to God and to get to know His heart.

In today's Scripture verse Jesus says, "No prayer is complete without repentance and reconciliation towards people who have hurt or offended us [or those we *feel* have offended us]. Don't come to God with unforgiveness and bitterness in your heart – it is not appropriate. He forgave all your sins, now do the same."

Comply with God on this matter. It's easy for people to sin, and bitterness comes just as easily. Walk the straight and narrow path with God and do what He says. It might knock your pride, but you will not regret it.

# ARROGANCE OR TRUTH?

*"I am the light of the world. Whoever follows Me will never walk in darkness, but will have the light of life."*
John 8:12

▶ Jesus is either arrogant and seriously misled, or correct and represents the Truth. He can either be rejected with contempt or worshiped with complete surrender. Either way, He leaves no room for compromise. With these words He will either be unmasked, or confirmed as the Son of God. Jesus' words are open to be tested.

That the world is covered in extreme darkness is a given. It's the only thing the media reports on. Small rays of light are rare. Is Jesus truly the light of the world? How can we test this? One way is to look at the lives of those who follow Him. Do they truly have the light of life?

Are you one of those followers? What does your life look like? Were you also in the dark at first and now have found the light that gives life? Witnessing about your faith is very important.

# A FAMILIAR VOICE

*"When the shepherd has brought out all his own, he goes on ahead of them, and his sheep follow him because they know his voice."*
John 10:4

▶ This metaphor was commonplace for the people in the Middle East. The shepherds didn't walk behind the sheep, herding them on; they walked in front and searched for grazing fields and shelter for the flock. The sheep didn't follow someone they weren't familiar with, because they didn't know them. They followed their shepherd because they knew his voice.

Followers of Jesus are like these sheep – not mindless, but familiar with their Shepherd's voice. They know what His voice sounds like. They can distinguish His voice among a hundred other voices. How? Firstly, because the Spirit of Christ is in them; secondly, because they spend a lot of time in His presence. There's no other way. They know His character and His voice, and He always remains the same.

Don't be satisfied with three minutes or a quick quiet time with Jesus. Make time to read His Word and meditate on it. Set aside time to hear what He is saying. Also do this together with other believers. Learn to distinguish His voice.

# TURN THE OTHER CHEEK

*"If someone slaps you on one cheek, turn to them the other also. If someone takes your coat, do not withhold your shirt from them."*
Luke 6:29

The more violent society becomes, the more difficult these words of Jesus are. The secret to this truth is actually much bigger than we think! Jesus' intention is not to say, "If you follow Me then you'll be a bunch of cowards." No, it's much greater! Jesus says, "You don't need to resist evil people. Leave them to Me. I will deal with them at the right time.

"Keep your hearts clean. Love others. Reject hatred and bitterness and resistance. I will judge righteously, purely and truthfully according to each person's deeds and actions. No one who acts without love will escape God's wrath. You don't have to fret about the unfairness and evil in the world. I will handle it."

Lord Jesus, I want to be completely free from the world's way of doing things. I desire Your value system more than anything else. Teach me to live exactly how You want me to. Amen.

# A TIP FROM THE MASTER CHEF

*"You are the salt of the earth. But if the salt loses its saltiness, how can it be made salty again? It is no longer good for anything, except to be thrown out and trampled underfoot."*
Matthew 5:13

Followers of Jesus have a big impact on the world around them because they are followers of Jesus – not because they're better than the rest. Because they follow Jesus and His life is in them, they bring flavor and meaning – this because of their connection to Jesus.

However, if they go about proclaiming Jesus' name without His light in their lives, they are worse than those living in darkness. Such people bring false hope. They let people follow them to receive hope, but let them turn back disappointed and in despair. Such testimonies are trampled on by the world.

Take great care when you identify yourself with Jesus and claim to be His follower. If you lose your integrity as His follower, it's very difficult to regain it in the eyes of the world.

# GREATER THAN DEATH

*Jesus said to her, "I am the resurrection and the life. The one who believes in Me will live, even though they die; and whoever lives by believing in Me will never die. Do you believe this?"*

John 11:25-26

Martha and Mary urgently called for Jesus. Their brother, Lazarus, was very sick. But Jesus didn't come on time. He came four days later. Lazarus was already dead.

Martha blamed Jesus and said, "If You came on time You could've saved him, but it's too late. He is dead" (see John 11:21). Jesus answered, "Martha, you think death is greater than I am. You believed in Me while your brother lived, but now you think that even I can't do anything about it. Martha, Someone greater than death is here!"

That was the most important lesson Martha and Mary had to learn. Nothing is impossible for Jesus, not even death. When Lazarus walked out of the grave, this truth was evident to all.

Don't limit Jesus. He's not just somebody. He is the Ruler of the universe! Is anything too big for Him? He is indeed who He said He is.

# SHORT AND SWEET

*"'Love the Lord your God with all your heart and with all your soul and with all your mind and with all your strength.'"*
Mark 12:30

For God life is all about relationships. When Jesus had the chance to sum up what it's all about in only a few words, this is what He said: "Friends, it's all about reconciliation and a relationship with God. All you need to do is to love God with everything you've got. That's the biggest life secret.

"Everything that aids you in this is called life. I give you this life. Don't think God is interested in religion. He couldn't be bothered by it. He is a God of the heart, and love and relationships. To know Him is the biggest joy any person can ever experience. Don't rob yourself of this joy and fulfillment."

Wonderful Father, my Father! I want to love You with all I've got. I don't want to withhold anything from You. If there is anything holding me back, please save me from it. I want to fully live the life You intended for me to live! Amen.

# THE LOGICAL CONSEQUENCE

*"The second is this: 'Love your neighbor as yourself.' There is no commandment greater than these."*
Mark 12:31

▶ The logical consequence of dedicated love towards God is love for other people. It's not possible to love God and at the same time walk around with hatred in your heart towards others.

These two aspects are inseparably linked. Respect and esteem for God are clearly evident in your respect and esteem for other people – *all* people. Even your enemies. It's impossible to love God and not do what pleases Him. Love for God means love for all the things that He loves.

God loves people. All people. God loves them so much that He'd give anything to save them from sin and death. You and I are living proof.

Holy Father, I realize there is something trying to steal my love for You: There are people in my life whom I struggle to love – I find I can't love them. Please show me how. Amen.

# THE NUTCRACKER

*Jesus looked at them and said,
"With man this is impossible, but
with God all things are possible."*
Matthew 19:26

When we hear or read these words we might think of a financial crisis, a difficult project or something similar. God can solve this impossible situation, right? Of course He can, but first of all Jesus is talking here about the salvation of people.

Some people's situation and salvation may seem impossible, but Jesus says that's not true. God can crack the hardest nut! When we give up with people, God never gives up. He is a greater and far better Evangelist than anyone on earth.

Sometimes it's a good thing to become despondent and give up on some people, because then God can do His work without us trying to intervene the whole time. God equals boundless love!

Father, Jesus taught me a wonderful lesson and He gives me hope. I surrender the hardest nut in my family and life unconditionally to You. Do Your humanly impossible work. I worship You in anticipation. Amen.

# ABSOLUTE FAITHFULNESS

*"If that is how God clothes the grass of the field, which is here today, and tomorrow is thrown into the fire, how much more will He clothe you – you of little faith!"*

Luke 12:28

Jesus reprimands the people for having little faith because they doubted that God would always be faithful. Such doubts often manifest as fear. Will we have enough? Will we have it on time? Will we be protected? Will God be with us? Jesus says, "God cares in great detail for the most elementary things in life, like the grass on the hill.

"Do you really think He will care for the grass but not for you, who are the crown of creation? Do you think so little of God and His character? Of course He will care for you! Just stay close to Him. Spend less time worrying about tomorrow and more time doing what God says."

Father, these words of Jesus comfort us. I confess out loud that You are completely faithful in Your care for me. May I thoroughly learn this lesson. Amen.

# THE GREATEST INVESTMENT

*Jesus said to them, "Go into all the world and preach the gospel to all creation."*
Mark 16:15

▶ "Go out – go in." How remarkable. Not only do these words of Jesus open up the heart of God to all nations, but it also says something significant of our everyday life. We easily create our own comfort zone where we feel protected and safe, and we isolate ourselves from what's happening around us.

Jesus, however, mobilizes His followers: "Move out of your comfort zone and safe places – and also from among each other. There's a whole world out there. You should not keep the gospel of God's grace to yourself. Move with it. Everywhere you find people, there's a need to be reconciled with God. Spread the blessing – always farther and wider. Don't be satisfied to only receive. Be like your Father and give!"

The greatest joy doesn't happen by protecting your own comfort, but by doing the will of Him who saved you and called you. Invest in His kingdom by doing what God asks of you.

# DISCIPLES, FOLLOWERS AND RUNNERS

*"This is My command:*
*Love each other."*
John 15:17

▶ Sometimes people act as if this command is just a polite recommendation – as if Jesus said, "Friends, if you feel like it and you're in a good mood, it would be very kind of you to please love other people – especially if the people aren't too weird."

One can conclude this from the way we react towards these words in our everyday lives. It's as if His command is optional – subject to conditions and our emotional energy. It's not true. This command is the dividing line between true disciples and comfortable followers. The followers quickly change into runners as soon as Jesus says something they don't like. How we acknowledge this command is how we acknowledge Jesus.

If Jesus is who He says He is, then this command is not a topic for discussion. It is a command of the King of kings. If you find it difficult, do not veto it. Ask for Jesus' help.

# A PROPER LESSON

*"If your brother or sister sins against you, rebuke them; and if they repent, forgive them. Even if they sin against you seven times in a day and seven times come back to you saying 'I repent,' you must forgive them."*
Luke 17:3-4

Do not reject and cut out people who have acted wrongly towards you. That's not how God treats us. To hurt others back doesn't teach them a lesson – it just cultivates more sin and lovelessness. Let Jesus teach them a lesson instead.

As a matter of fact, our joy is a result of God forgiving our sins and being willing to build a relationship with us, even while He knows about the possible disappointments on the way from our side. If you're a follower of Jesus, you're a child of the Father. Do what He does, live like He lives. That's the best way of "teaching someone a lesson," because you open the way for God to deal with them.

Every time you're tempted to say, "But how can I forgive these people?" think about how God forgives you. Ask Him to show you how to forgive. He will gladly teach you!

# LIKE FATHER, LIKE SON

*"Blessed are the peacemakers, for they will be called children of God."*
Matthew 5:9

Why would peacemakers be called children of God? Because they are like God. That's who God is. In Matthew 5:44-45, Jesus says, "But I tell you, love your enemies and pray for those who persecute you, that you may be children of your Father in heaven."

That's how you distinguish between children of the world (the devil) and the children of God. Who are they like? Whose desires do they fulfill? Are they peacemakers or peace-takers? Do they build or destroy relationships? Do they forgive or do they embitter? Whose nature do they reveal? Do they protect or do they chase away?

A wonderful blessing rests on God's children, but on the children of the world rests a blistering curse.

If you take these words seriously, you take God seriously. God the Father doesn't raise terrorists – not even emotional or spiritual terrorists. He is the Wonderful Counselor, Mighty God, Everlasting Father, Prince of Peace (see Isa. 9:6).

# AN OUTSTANDING PROMOTION

*"Those who exalt themselves will be humbled, and those who humble themselves will be exalted."*
Matthew 23:12

The biggest promotion in life comes when you side with God. People can fire you and write you off, but a person who lives consistently with their heart and life, is a person who catches the eye of the Executive Director and Founder of the universe. Pride is a lifestyle and attitude that differs from God.

Your incompetence is revealed every time you differ from God. In the same way, your competence is revealed every time you agree with God and submit to His authority. Don't disqualify yourself from being promoted by thinking you know better than God. When He says, "Jump!" ask not "Why?" but "How high?"

Father, I grew up in a world where everything stands in opposition to You. If these worldly values still reside in my heart, please show them to me so that I can repent of them. There is no one like You! Amen.

# THE MOST WONDERFUL FATHER

*"Your Father knows what you need before you ask Him."*
Matthew 6:8

These words are a great source of comfort. The mere words "your Father" are comfort enough. I don't know what your relationship with your earthly father is or was, but I know that God the Father is far greater! He is a true Father.

His love and care are without sin and defect. With Him you never need feel embarrassed or have to perform to be loved and highly esteemed. You just need to be with Him. He's also not indifferent towards you. He knows you like the palm of His hand. You have no reason to distrust Him. He loves you and He cares for you – far more than you can imagine.

Never allow the violator of character and the master of lies to make you believe anything else about God the Father. Jesus knows what He's talking about. He is close to the Father's heart.

# MOTHS AND COCKROACHES

*"Everyone who does evil hates the light, and will not come into the light for fear that their deeds will be exposed."*
John 3:20

▶ If someone would ask you what you are, a moth or a cockroach, you'd wonder what they were up to. Think about it: Moths can handle a light. If it's on, they hurry towards it. Cockroaches, in turn, can't get away from the light fast enough. Jesus says people act in the same way when God's light shines.

The pure in heart run towards the light. Those who are unclean run away from it. You see this happen everywhere, especially in court. People pay a lot of money to hide what they've done and spend lots of energy lying about the truth. That's the behavior of a cockroach. What do *you* do? Children of God have a particular fondness for light. Light doesn't threaten them, it attracts them.

Light draws a clear line between those who side with God and those who oppose Him. His light reveals the condition of the heart. Are you running away or running toward the light? You be the judge.

# THE FOUNTAIN OF LIFE

*"Everyone who drinks this water will be thirsty again, but whoever drinks the water I give them will never thirst. Indeed, the water I give them will become in them a spring of water welling up to eternal life."*

John 4:13-14

Nothing that the world offers can quench your thirst. You continuously have to keep drinking in order to carry on in the world. Even though the world's water has many labels, it's still unable to truly quench your thirst.

There are many extremely thirsty people out there. Jesus offers the alternative. What He gives refreshes the soul. You can drink as much as you want. It will heal and cleanse you. Not only will this water quench your eternal thirst, but it will also change you into a fountain for other thirsty souls. This fountain gives life. Jesus' water is godly and supernatural, and it's evident in the results.

The water of the world has been designed to keep you thirsty. God is focused on quenching your thirst. Do not drink from the wrong fountain – it will rob you of your life.

# GOD WILL AMAZE YOU

*"Let the little children come to Me, and do not hinder them, for the kingdom of God belongs to such as these."*
Mark 10:14

"Such as these." What does that mean? Simple: Children are uncomplicated and defenseless, though not without sin. The kingdom of God is not reserved for super stars, rich people, the mighty and self-made people. Jesus says, "Don't chase the children away like they don't belong here.

"I *want* to *see* and *hear* them. I'm not too important or the Kingdom too superior. It's the children who are the receptive ones. They're not out of place – in fact, to be with Me is their place. Do not think that God's teachings and ministry are just for adults or advanced people. Bring them, and see what God can accomplish through them. You'll be amazed. God will amaze you."

Lord, sometimes I feel left out from important things and I even shut people out. Please help me to never lose the simplicity of a child. Amen.

# EVIL – RATIFIED OR DESTROYED?

*"To you who are listening I say: Love your enemies, do good to those who hate you, bless those who curse you, pray for those who mistreat you."*
Luke 6:27-28

▶ With these words Jesus revealed the Father's character. Everything Jesus said and did was aimed at revealing the heart of God to people. No one can do it better than Him, because He and the Father are one.

"If you've seen Me, you've seen the Father," Jesus once said to His disciples (see John 14:9). God's kingdom differs completely from the world. Don't fall for the selfish and evil wisdom of the world. It will only lead to destruction.

Become part of God's world. It might seem senseless to you, but it is the healing and saving wisdom of God. Nothing can compare to it. God's character is not futile, but powerful to destroy the darkness.

Our lives will either ratify or destroy darkness. If you believe in God as omnipotent and almighty, let your reaction to evil reflect this fact. God knows what He's about.

# FEBRUARY

# SMALL THINGS WITH A GREAT SURPRISE

*"Are not two sparrows sold for a penny? Yet not one of them will fall to the ground outside your Father's care."*
Matthew 10:29

God's omnipotence is often revealed most in the small things. We look at big things and say, "Wow, God is great!", but often the seemingly insignificant things reveal His indescribable and incomprehensible greatness more.

One sees this in the smallest, most fragile flower that you step on every day. One observes it in the way God cares for the things we don't even bat an eye over. Sparrows – what are they worth? Poor people bought two sparrows for a penny as an offering to God (where rich people sacrificed a lamb, goats or even cows). We might look down on such an offering, but God doesn't think it is inferior. He reigns over the smallest things with the same power and glory that He displays over the "big" things.

Father, Your greatness is indescribable when I notice the small things in life. Help me to see You for who You really are, and not for who I think You are. Amen.

# RECEIVE WHAT YOU GIVE

*"Give, and it will be given to you.
A good measure, pressed down,
shaken together and running over,
will be poured into your lap. For with
the measure you use, it will be
measured to you."*
Luke 6:38

I've heard people use these words of Jesus to imply that if you give money, God will give it back to you twofold. But that's not what Jesus is saying here. Firstly, it's not God who is doing the primary "giving back," but people, and secondly, Jesus is talking about judgment and forgiveness.

He says, "Friends, don't walk around with judgment and bitterness in your hearts. Forgive. If you walk around with a judgmental spirit and hand out bitterness to everyone, you will receive double the amount back, but if you live with a forgiving heart you'll receive the same back from people – with interest!

Work it out. What do you prefer: criticism and judgment, or forgiveness? Give to others what you desire for yourself and it will come your way."

The principle of "treat others like you want to be treated" stands firm. It's a valuable lesson and Jesus knows what He's talking about. Nobody likes to be judged and criticized, so don't give it out to others either!

# A LIFE THAT GLORIFIES GOD

*"In the same way, let your light shine before others, that they may see your good deeds and glorify your Father in heaven."*
Matthew 5:16

"Let your light shine" doesn't mean "let your left hand know what your right hand is doing." It rather means that whatever we say and do, it should glorify the Father and not embarrass Him. Children of light are meticulously watched by those who hide in darkness.

Darkness is always looking for a rod to punish the light in order to defend its own darkness. Jesus says, "Don't give darkness a reason to punish you. Live a righteous life, live in love. Even if darkness is always searching for a reason to hurt you, he won't find one [except for senseless arguments, of course]. A holy life confirms God's truth and glorifies Him."

Living a life in the light is the best way of worship. Don't restrict your worship to church services and worship sessions. Let your whole life be worship to God.

# STOP, THIEF!

*"Some people are like seed along
the path, where the word is sown.
As soon as they hear it, Satan comes
and takes away the word that was
sown in them."*
Mark 4:15

Before you start thinking about who these people are
that Jesus' words refer to, examine your own life first. It is
possible that these words are applicable to you and me.
Jesus says something and it might not suit us. It might be
uncomfortable or unusual, and we would rather let them
pass. That's how Satan wants to steal the Word from our
lives.

All the things that we hear but don't act on are at risk
of being stolen. That's a great danger. We live in a society that is much more focused on collecting information
than on applying it. For the Word of God to be stolen
from your life is much more serious than your possessions
being stolen. Protect God's words with your life!

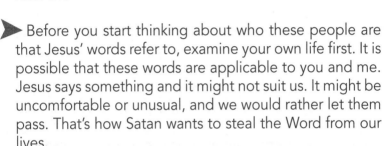

Lord Jesus, please help me to focus on doing and keeping
Your Word and Spirit in my heart. I want Your words to bear
fruit in my life and give life in return. Amen.

# PRAY AND BE TRANSFORMED

*Jesus told them, "The harvest is plentiful, but the workers are few. Ask the Lord of the harvest, therefore, to send out workers into His harvest field."*

Luke 10:2

Again Jesus knows what He's talking about. A strange thing happens when I pray to "the Lord of the harvest to send out workers into His harvest field". Deep in my soul I become focused on the harvest. The more I pray, the more my eyes are opened to the great harvest around me.

We are taught from an early age to focus on ourselves, but Jesus quickly puts this twisted perception straight. There is nothing better than to look and see the same things that Jesus sees. It brings depth and power to our lives that is evident through our value system. In this way ordinary lives become meaningful – even legendary – in the eyes of God.

Lord to whom the harvest belongs, open my eyes to see the things You see. Elevate my soul to see the bigger picture instead of digging around in the dirt. Mobilize me to do what You want me to do! Amen.

# YOUR IDENTITY DOCUMENT

*"By this everyone will know that you are My disciples, if you love one another."*
John 13:35

The world can imitate anything you can think of, but it can't imitate true love. Although the world tries its best, the difference between genuine and fake is obvious. It's one thing that can only be raised by the Spirit of God.

It's also the one thing that distinguishes the followers of Jesus from others. Without it you're without identification. Without it you can't prove that you follow Jesus.

To submit to Jesus' authority means to love others – including your enemies. The two can't be separated. Do not diminish your testimony as a disciple of Jesus by falling for a life without love. Protect your identity – protect your testimony.

Lord Jesus, I understand now why Satan so badly wants me to live with bitterness and lovelessness in my heart. Help me to throw off the burdens of selfishness and a lack of love so that others can see whom I follow. Amen.

# THE KING IS WITH YOU

*"Take courage! It is I.
Don't be afraid."*
Matthew 14:27

▶ Jesus is quoted as saying many times, "Do not be afraid." Angels are recorded in the Bible as saying the same thing. The meaning behind this is greater than we think. In actual fact what Jesus was saying is, "There is no reason for you to be afraid, because I'm here. I'm with you.

"Even if you're taken away to be killed, I'm still with you. The One who is greater than death is here. The One who is bigger than crises and evil is here! Let your heart be still and relax. Why all this fear? It's not necessary. I'm your Shepherd and I'll guide you in the steps of justice leading to rest and peace. Nothing is out of control. I'm in control!"

Jesus' words are not intended to only mean "stop being afraid", but rather "see Me!", the King is with you!

# LET GO
# AND UNLOAD

*"It is easier for a camel to go through the eye of a needle than for someone who is rich to enter the kingdom of God."*
Mark 10:25

The "eye of the needle" has been claimed to be a gate in Jerusalem (actually a big door). When camels came to the city with merchandise, the owner had to offload everything from the camel's back in order for the camel to pass through the gate. The camel couldn't pass through any other way.

Jesus says, "People who have collected many material possessions find it difficult to focus their hearts on something more important. They are too scared of losing something, and enter the kingdom of God very reluctantly. They want what God has to offer as long as all the things they've collected are not jeopardized. They don't want to unpack and let go. That's often their biggest stumbling block." One cannot enter God's kingdom this way.

In God's kingdom He is the King and everyone else does what He says. To come with your own terms and conditions is to deny God His rule. It won't work. Will you choose God even if you must offload?

# GOD'S FISHERMAN

*"Don't be afraid; from now on you will fish for people."*
Luke 5:10

These words are so significant! Simon was a fisherman. It was his source of income. That's what he was good at. It's a world he understood and where he could express himself. Jesus says, "Mr Fisherman, don't be afraid of finding yourself in a place where you'll feel meaningless. You're a fisherman, and a good one.

"You're still going to be a fisherman, but God is going to broaden your horizons and your fishing. Be a fisherman, Peter, but be one on God's level. It's far greater than you can imagine. Throw out your net and your fishing line, but do it God's way. You're going to reel people in, Peter – boats and boats filled with people!"

What is your gift? What makes you excited? For Peter it was fishing. God made you that way and He wants to use you in a bigger area. Don't be afraid.

# THE LOVE TEST

*"If you love Me, keep My commands."*
John 14:15

To love God is to submit to His authority. Being rebellious is unloving and no reason to boast. There are many reasons why we may say we love Jesus: our income, church involvement, being accepted in our social circle.

The test of the sincerity of our love lies in fact in our submissiveness to Jesus. It will either affirm our testimony or disprove it. And what better way to test our obedience than to say, "Love others."

All of Jesus' commands can be summed up with these words. Show your love, not through songs and empty words, but through your actions. That's one of the most important evangelical tools.

We live in a society focused on comfort and making things "easy." Obedience doesn't take any of that into account. Only Jesus and His truth are important.

# GOD REWARDS OBEDIENCE

*"When you give to the needy, do not announce it with trumpets, as the hypocrites do in the synagogues and on the streets, to be honored by others. Truly I tell you, they have received their reward in full."*

Matthew 6:2

The reason Jesus said, "Do not let your left hand know what your right hand is doing" (v. 3), becomes clear in today's Scripture verse. What strikes one here is that goodwill is indeed rewarded. What we do to others in goodwill will be rewarded by God. A part of the reward is that we'll also reap love. The most important part is that our obedience will strengthen and deepen our relationship with God.

Disobedience obstructs our relationship, but obedience builds it up. The more we get to know God, the greater His glory becomes in our lives. The recognition of people may be minimal, but God's recognition stretches into eternity. Hypocrisy is not only offensive, but also robs us of true glory.

People will sell their souls for other people's recognition. That's an expensive price to pay for nothing! Anchor yourself in God's heart. His recognition brings unquenchable life.

# DON'T HARDEN YOUR HEART

*"What do you think? If a man owns a hundred sheep, and one of them wanders away, will he not leave the ninety-nine on the hills and go to look for the one that wandered off?"*
Matthew 18:12

What do you think? The answer to Jesus' question is logical. If a shepherd would go to such great lengths for a replaceable sheep, how much more would God not make an effort with a lost, irreplaceable soul? No person will be lost by accident. It requires persistent and diligent resistance against God's grace to become separated from God for eternity.

His zeal was already disclosed when He sent Jesus to die for us, and His zeal is still visible on a daily basis in the effort He makes to win people's hearts. Still, there are people, despite everything that God does, who harden their hearts. For them the dreadful day will come when God will eventually hand them over to their stubbornness. Who will save them then?

Let us not harden our hearts when God speaks (see Heb. 4:7). God's grace and mercy lead us to repentance (see Rom. 2:4-5). Hardened hearts embrace death.

# DO NOT DISREGARD THE GOSPEL

*"What is the kingdom of God like? What shall I compare it to? It is like a mustard seed, which a man took and planted in his garden. It grew and became a tree, and the birds perched in its branches."*

Luke 13:18-19

The Gospel of Jesus Christ might sound like nonsense for those who are perishing (see 1 Cor. 1:18), but to those who are being saved it is indeed the power of God. It might be small and insignificant, but the result is astronomical!

It might start small and fragile in a person's life, but it will grow to victory in God over sin, giving life and refreshment. The body of Christ might have started off with twelve disciples, but it swept over the world like wildfire. People might dismiss it, but it can conquer and destroy the kingdom of darkness. Do not despise the little works of God – they have the godly ability to transform and renew.

Thank You, Father, for every area in my life where You are involved, no matter how small. Your "little works" grow to great power and glory. Thank You for working in me. Amen.

# BE ACCOUNTABLE

*"If anyone causes one of these little ones – those who believe in Me – to stumble, it would be better for them if a large millstone were hung around their neck and they were thrown into the sea."*
Mark 9:42

To harden your own heart to God's goodness is a terrible tragedy, but to turn someone away from the heart of God is an indescribable tragedy. Jesus says it is better to drown than to do this. If God rewards and blesses even the smallest deed of kindness, He will also deal with this horror accordingly.

To let others stumble is no small matter. With this and other matters on his mind, the writer of Hebrews said, "It is a dreadful thing to fall into the hands of the living God" (Heb. 10:31). We won't only give account for our own lives one day, but also for what we've done in other people's lives, be it good or bad.

Live responsibly, with respect for God, and be accountable. Weigh your words and deeds. Don't treat life with indifference.

# FAITH SAVES

*"Whoever believes in Him is not condemned, but whoever does not believe stands condemned already because they have not believed in the name of God's one and only Son."*
John 3:18

Jesus' words in John are extremely important. It will do you well to read the whole passage and meditate and pray on it. To believe in Jesus is to believe that He is who He says He is, and *to respond to it*. This saves us from being condemned.

Everyone who embraces the Son and submits to Jesus' authority will never stand condemned. But to reject Him literally means that the pronouncing judgment is already written – God must just sign. Everything God offers us to save us from sin and judgment is in Jesus. Everything that causes us to be judged lies outside Jesus.

Where are you today? Are you *in* Jesus, a disciple obedient to His authority? Then you're free from God's wrath. Hallelujah! If you're not, then this is God's invitation to you. Don't delay.

# REPENTANCE LEADS TO SALVATION

*"Blessed are those who mourn, for they will be comforted."*
Matthew 5:4

There are two reactions to sin. The one is to feel remorse before God about what you've done, and the other is to regret that you've been caught out. Needless to say, the latter is not true repentance; rather, it is self-pity. The former leads to repentance and being saved, and salvation brings forgiveness and deliverance. It brings comfort and healing.

To only mourn brings no comfort, but to mourn and look for comfort at Jesus' feet will give you unparalleled comfort. This comfort will not only happen one day when we see Him eye to eye, but in this life too. It's part of "taste and see that the Lord is good" (Ps. 34:8). A sincere heart will always find God!

Jesus' ministry as a Comforter is very real and tangible. Why would anyone not want to take shelter with Him? This question resounds throughout the ages as well as today, to you and me.

# THE APPEARANCE OF HYPOCRISY

*"When you pray, do not be like the hypocrites, for they love to pray standing in the synagogues and on the street corners to be seen by others. Truly I tell you, they have received their reward in full."*
Matthew 6:5

Hypocrisy means to pretend to be submissive to God's authority. There are few things that offend as badly as pretence. People the world over dislike it. To pretend that you have a relationship with God so that other people can think you're wonderful and exemplary offends God.

Not only is it reprehensible, but it also withholds the person who pretends from a real encounter with God. For many people religion means serving people. They go to church and serve to be esteemed in people's eyes (and it might be good for business too). Such behavior can be very damaging to the testimonies of the gospel in the world. Throw it out like dirty water!

Father, show me where I'm being hypocritical. Do I pretend to stand under Your authority, but don't act accordingly? Reveal it to me so that I can turn away from it. Amen.

# THE RICH BECOME RICHER

*Jesus replied, "I tell you that to every one who has, more will be given, but as for the one who has nothing, even what they have will be taken away."*
Luke 19:26

▶ Read the preceding Scripture passage to understand what Jesus is talking about (see also Luke 8). Jesus isn't talking about riches or possessions, but about the revelation of God. Those who listen to God and obey Him will be enriched in knowledge and the revelation of God. But those who do not heed to God's words will also lose the little they think they know.

This was especially applicable to the Jews: not listening and doing what Jesus said deprived them of the little they thought they knew about God. The more you listen and do, the richer you'll become in the true knowledge of God. The less you do, the poorer you'll become.

Don't be careless with what you've heard Jesus say. Do it – even if you don't understand everything. By doing, your understanding will increase and your knowledge of God will deepen.

# A GREAT PANTRY

*"Do not work for food that spoils, but for food that endures to eternal life, which the Son of Man will give you. For on Him God the Father has placed His seal of approval."*
John 6:27

Jesus doesn't mean not working, but rather working smarter. Think about the time and effort we spend on providing for our families. All of us get hungry again and the toil and reward of our work quickly disappear. If we then work so diligently for things that disappear so rapidly, how much more should we not work for things that last. It's common sense!

There are foods that will not only satisfy our bodies, but also our soul, and give eternal life. Don't let this pass you by. Providing for your basic needs is important, but eternal provision is far more important. The only place to find it is with Jesus.

Don't relax in your zeal to provide for your family, but also fervently chase after the food that Jesus gives. It yields the best results for your time and energy.

# OUR WONDERFUL ROLE MODEL

*"I have set you an example that you should do as I have done for you."*
John 13:15

How thankful I am for all the role models I have had in my life, men and women I look up to, to complement my own shortcomings and character when I need it most. Amongst these people are legends. Not because they're famous or prominent, but because they demonstrate that Jesus is the best Role Model.

Their influence in my life is great. When your role models and heroes demonstrate and proclaim that Jesus is their Role Model and Hero, great power can be drawn from them! What a wonderful Role Model is Jesus! There is none like Him. His life shines like a light in the darkness. What an honor to have Him as our Leader!

Jesus is the perfect Role Model. Imitate Him in everything. If the world can follow and imitate their role models shamelessly, why would we tread lightly around Jesus? His life is our example – follow Him!

# EVEN BETTER THAN BEFORE

*"I will ask the Father, and He will give you another advocate to help you and be with you forever – the Spirit of truth. The world cannot accept Him, because it neither sees Him nor knows Him. But you know Him, for He lives with you and will be in you."*
John 14:16-17

These words are from Jesus' last conversation with His disciples before He was arrested and sentenced. His disciples were ready to sink into a deep depression and abandonment after everything Jesus said, when suddenly the following words followed:

"My friends, do not lose hope! Do you think God will make this big effort to get you excited and then just leave you in the desert? No, brothers! That's not how He operates. I'm going back to the Father, but God will send His Spirit to be with you forever. He will be with you and will lead you to the whole truth about God in everything that comes your way. I was with you for three years, but through God's Spirit I'll be with you for all eternity."

Father, make me sensitive to Your Spirit in me and with me. May my eyes be opened to see the way to Your truth in everything I do. Amen.

# PUT IN EVERYTHING

*"They all gave out of their wealth; but she, out of her poverty, put in everything – all she had to live on."*
Mark 12:44

▶ The word "everything" depicts the complete focus and dedication. "Give your all!" says the coach to his athlete, in other words, "Focus, and be 100% dedicated to the race ahead." Many people are slightly committed, but slightly committed means not being dedicated at all.

The Pharisees gave generously out of their wealth to the temple. It might seem like a big thing, but in God's eyes it was small, because their hearts were not committed to Him. The poor woman didn't give much, but she gave with a completely committed heart. God celebrates over it! He rejoices and is glad because of her, because her focus is on Him alone. God will strengthen her (see 2 Chron. 16:9) and her reward will be great. The only thing that will be great for the hypocritical Pharisees will be their disillusionment and embarrassment.

Don't be fooled by show and "performance." It's not real. God looks at the heart. May that which He sees in you and me be absolute dedication. He will strengthen us.

# IMPOSSIBLE RIGHTEOUSNESS

*"I tell you that unless your righteousness surpasses that of the Pharisees and the teachers of the law, you will certainly not enter the kingdom of heaven."*
Matthew 5:20

▶ Initially these words sound impossible. Who could keep the law better than the Pharisees and teachers of the law? Nobody will then be able to enter into the kingdom of heaven! But Jesus hits the nail – as always – on the head. "The law says you shall not commit adultery, but I tell you that if you merely look at a man or woman and desire them outside God's limits, you've already done it"(see Matt. 5:27-28).

Jesus' words even caught the Pharisees off guard. The purity that Jesus brings is not a legalistic lifestyle, but a deep cleansing of the heart. To keep the laws on the surface means nothing, but to be freed from sins deep within your soul means everything. Only such people will enter the kingdom of heaven – without it, it's impossible!

Religion is concerned about the rights and wrongs in the finest detail, but the gospel of Jesus is concerned about salvation and the cleansing of the heart. Embrace the gospel!

# THE STATUS QUO

*"Enter through the narrow gate. For wide is the gate and broad is the road that leads to destruction, and many enter through it."*
Matthew 7:13

Paul calls it the "ways of this world" (Eph. 2:2) – the *status quo*. There are two cultures, two systems, two lifestyles on earth. The one is the culture, system and way of life of the world without God. All people are born into this way of life and grow up in a worldly culture and system. All people act, talk and live the same way.

The other culture, system and way of life belong to God. It's completely different. No one can please God according to the world's way of living; it is the road that leads to destruction. To be part of God's culture, system and way of life means to get away from the ways of the world, and Jesus is the gate.

Maintain God's *status quo*. With Him is life and peace. He will teach you His culture and system. No one can walk on both roads – it's either God's way or the world's way. Choose one today.

# AN APPROACHABLE GOD

*"Ask and it will be given to you; seek and you will find; knock and the door will be opened to you."*
Matthew 7:7

Jesus says, "Ask God to cleanse your hearts and He will do it. Seek His face and you'll find it. Knock on the door of God's kingdom and He will open it for you. That's why I came. The opportunity to ask, seek and knock is here!"

Nobody can ask God to cleanse their heart without acknowledging that they are unclean before God. No one can approach God without proclaiming that we are all far removed from God. God has said, "Return to Me … and I will return to you" (Zech. 1:3).

No one can knock on the door of God's kingdom without acknowledging that they have no part in it. God will give all these things without blame.

Thank You, Father, that the way to Your heart is open. Thank You for being available and approachable to receive me. Thank You for embracing me and making me a part of Your family. Thank You for cleansing me. Amen.

# A CHAMPION GRAPE FARMER

*"I am the true vine, and My Father is the gardener."*
John 15:1

It's not only the interaction and cooperation that strike people, but also the Father's involvement in the growth of the body of Christ. Jesus is the Vine from which all life comes. The branches are those who are grafted in Jesus through faith.

The Father is the Farmer who monitors and does everything He can with great intensity to ensure that the vineyard is fertile and healthy. The Father definitely doesn't watch from a distance; He's hand's on! To allow the Father to do His will in your life is the best way to grow and bear fruit. To be in Jesus is the only way to be part of God's farm.

The gospel is very simple. It is our fancies, pride and self-centeredness that complicate things. Allow God to prune and shape you according to His will. When the time for harvest comes, you won't regret it!

# A CONTINUAL FEAST

*"In the same way, I tell you, there is rejoicing in the presence of the angels of God over one sinner who repents."*
Luke 15:10

Salvation is a matter of great joy. How can it be anything else? Sin leads to complete destruction, but the Father has given His Son to ensure complete healing. Each person who accepts this offer from God causes great joy in heaven.

Another person conquers darkness through Jesus. Another person has moved from death to life. One more person who was far removed from God is now a part of His family. One more person confirms that God is good and true. Another has found their purpose in life. And it's one more person who has broken away from Satan's slavery and become an heir of God.

Salvation is no small matter. The person who has been saved is also not insignificant.

Does the above situation describe your new status in God? Know that God rejoices over you! Your new life is much greater than you can imagine.

# TO TRULY GLORIFY GOD

*"If you love those who love you,
what reward will you get? Are not
even the tax collectors doing that?"*
Matthew 5:46

It's the easier way out, although it's still hard. Just to love those who love you is already a challenge – just look at the state of marriages nowadays. That's the way of the world. Love those who love you, but the rest, beware! God's way is completely different. Jesus says, "You think it's great to love those who love you, but that's nothing. Even evil people do that.

"To love those who love you and especially to love those who don't love you back – that's worth mentioning. Who can do that? The people who stand under God's authority. God will rejoice and reward them. They proclaim God's truth and glorify Him."

Lord Jesus, I don't just want You to help me love others, but also to prevent me from withholding love in my life. May God's truth and life consume me. Amen.

# AN EXTRAORDINARY LIFE

*"If you greet only your own people, what are you doing more than others? Do not even pagans do that?"*
Matthew 5:47

The King James Bible says, "If ye salute your brethren only, what do ye more than others?" It is indeed no particularly exceptional lifestyle, yet God called us to lead an extraordinary life. What is your definition of an extraordinary life? God's definition is simple:

An extraordinary life is to be loving and respectful towards all people – even those (and especially those) who are not loving and respectful towards you. That's special, because it's completely against the flow of the world. It's extraordinary because only those with the Spirit of God in them can get this right. They not only get it right, but it's their usual, everyday way of living. You can't fake it – it won't last! You have it because you live through the Spirit. That's that.

The world has no respect for this truth, because the world has no respect for God. But we have! We don't want anything else but to live through God's Spirit. It will show in the way we love.

# MARCH

# INTENSE FRICTIONS

*"Do not suppose that I have come to bring peace to the earth. I did not come to bring peace, but a sword. For I have come to turn 'a man against his father, a daughter against her mother, a daughter-in-law against her mother-in-law – a man's enemies will be the members of his own household.'"*

Matthew 10:34-36

Many people struggle with the words from today's Scripture passage, especially those who want to reject Jesus' claim on their lives. How can the "King of Peace" say such things? Easy. Have you seen what happens when someone surrenders their life to Jesus? Their friends distance themselves and their family becomes hostile. Why? Because darkness hates the light.

For instance, a man who lives in the darkness can't stand it when God's light shines in his wife's life. This causes intense friction. The world is full of stories like this. There is solidarity between people in the darkness and reconciliation between people living in the light. But there is always resistance between dark and light.

Make sure that the friction between light and dark is not as a result of you being unloving or unwise. Don't give darkness any reason to hold you back. Stay in the light and life of Christ.

# A FRUIT EXPERT

*"By their fruit you will recognize them. Do people pick grapes from thornbushes, or figs from thistles?"*
Matthew 7:16

Your lifestyle reveals your standing in life. Through your life it becomes evident under whose authority you stand. You either stand under the world and Satan's rule, or you stand under God in the kingdom of His Son. People can say whatever they want, but their lives identify "the tree."

Identification says, "This is a peach tree, because the tree bears peaches." Judgment says, "This is a tomato and not a peach; cut it off." Identification says, "This tree belongs to the rest of the fruit trees." Judgment says, "Destroy it!" Jesus enables you to become a fruit expert, but He alone is the Judge. Look after your fruit. Bear fruit that is evident of your conversion (see Matt. 3:8).

Your testimony is tested against the fruit that you bear. We will have to give an account of the integrity of our testimony before God one day – then He will judge accordingly.

# AN UNCLEAN HEART

*"What comes out of a person is what defiles them."*
Mark 7:20

Legalism is very much concerned with the outward appearance. People have developed it into a fine art. From it, thousands of laws and rules are borne to supposedly keep people from impurity. Jesus keeps it simple: "Impurity comes from the heart, not through other things. It doesn't make sense to 'cleanse' your outward appearance while the source of your uncleanness stays unaffected."

It might fool people, but it doesn't fool God. God doesn't care about outward demonstrations. He is focused on what goes on in your heart. His cleansing is profound and in truth – it's not a smokescreen for legalism. Do you want to please God? Let Him cleanse your heart for true holiness.

Don't confuse legalism with God. God is not the author of it, but rather people. Run away from it! There is no life or salvation in outward religious piousness.

# LOVING AND WISE

*"A new command I give you: Love one another. As I have loved you, so you must love one another."*
John 13:34

▶ The summary of everything that God desires and everything that He is, is revealed through these words. Do you want to know what you may and may not do? Ask yourself this question: Which things are loving and wise, and which are not?

Review your whole life – the way you dress, spend your money, how you walk and talk, your attitude and reactions – are they loving and wise towards others, or selfish and unwise? The joke that you want to tell – is it wise and loving? Your attitude towards your wife or mother-in-law – is it loving and wise? Your reaction towards your teenager – is it loving and wise?

That is the command under which Jesus' disciples stand. Nothing else. Nothing else is needed.

Father, cleanse me through Your Spirit in everything towards love and wisdom. In many areas I am unwise and without love, without even realizing it. I want to stand under Your authority with everything I have. Amen.

# DEEP COMFORT

*Jesus told him, "Don't be afraid; just believe."*
Mark 5:36

To believe means so much more than we think. That's also the reason why we need not be afraid or upset. We don't believe in faith alone. We believe that Jesus is who He said He is, and that He can do what He said He can. Nothing can change that.

No matter how dark and scary the storm or circumstances or what our emotions tell us, Jesus is still who He said He is. Therein lies our comfort. Even if we walk through the valley of death, yet our Shepherd is with us – He watches over us (see Ps. 23:4). If you don't believe that, then you have all the reason in the world to be afraid!

Preserve your faith in the integrity of Jesus. If you get robbed of it, you are subject to the lies of the devil. Jesus is as faithful as He is God.

# FALSE FAITH

*"Very truly I tell you, you are looking for Me, not because you saw the signs I performed but because you ate the loaves and had your fill."*
John 6:26

➤ Was the multiplication of bread not a miracle? Jesus is actually saying, "The miracles that I perform are to reveal to you that I am the Messiah – the Son of the living God. You're not looking for Me because you saw the signs and believed. You're only searching for Me because it seems like I can make your lives comfortable.

"You think I'm some sort of wizard who can solve problems that most of you battle with. That's not faith! That's greed … for a more comfortable life. That's not the faith that I want to establish in your hearts. Such faith is worth nothing. Wait until I do something you don't like – then you'll see for yourselves what I see now."

Are you prepared to worship Jesus as Lord and God, even if He doesn't do what you ask?

# IT'S TIME TO REST

*"Come to Me, all you who are weary and burdened, and I will give you rest."*
Matthew 11:28

In the Scripture verse Jesus speaks about people who are heavily burdened by sins and formalism. Both of these cause burdens and wounds that life forces out of you. "Weary and burdened" describes the situation very well! In opposition to sin and formalism stands Jesus. He is the only One who can free you and give you rest. Nowhere else do we find those things that we so desperately long for.

Jesus invites us, but our answer is in our own hands. Will we accept or muddle along? Maybe things will get better? Never! It only gets worse. Now why would people then not accept Jesus' invitation? Do you know?

Do you long for rest? Accept Jesus' invitation. Allow Him to free you. Don't wait to see what the rest are doing. Nobody is going to take responsibility for your exhaustion. Take hold of Jesus with all you have.

# AN UNTHINKABLE CONNECTION

*"This is My body given for you; do this in remembrance of Me."*
Luke 22:19

▶ To be part of the body of Christ is awesome! Your connection with Jesus in this way is so unique and wonderful that it was almost unthinkable in centuries before. It's impossible to "belong" anywhere more than this.

Not only is your connection to Jesus indescribable, but also your connection to everyone else who is connected to Him. Our fellow allies might look plain and unimportant, but nothing is further from the truth! They are also part of the body of Jesus. We have nothing but love and respect for them. We can't but love them, because our love and respect for Jesus knows no bounds.

Don't see yourself or fellow believers as insignificant. Your connection and commitment to Christ is the miracle of the ages! Be gracious and respectful. Serve Jesus. No one can break your connection to Him.

# AN AUTHORITATIVE VOICE

*"No one can serve two masters. Either you will hate the one and love the other, or you will be devoted to the one and despise the other. You cannot serve both God and money."*

Matthew 6:24

This is Jesus' striking explanation about the kingdom of darkness and the Kingdom of Light. You can only belong to one of them. There can be no dual citizenship. In this way it's easy to distinguish which kingdom you belong to. Whose values and words do you regard as more important? Jesus uses money as an example to depict the kingdom of the world. Money is not only a currency, but a power.

This power is not part of God's kingdom, but the kingdom of darkness. Do you stand under the authority of money or God's power? You can't serve both. To use money is one thing, but to stand under its authority is something completely different.

Are you scared of what you might lose if you choose God? That's how the power of money speaks to you. Its voice is deep and authoritative, but does it have enough power to dethrone God? You choose.

# MORE POWER THAN SUPERMAN

*"Everything is possible for one who believes."*
Mark 9:23

▶ I've heard these words being quoted in many forms. Mostly people mean, "You can succeed in anything if you just believe." That's not what Jesus is saying here. Jesus says, "You ask if I can help you? If you believe in your heart that I am who I said I am and that I can do what I promised, you'll understand what is possible and what not.

"Of course I can cleanse your heart. Of course I can heal you. I'm the Son of the Living God! If you don't lose sight of who I am, you'll even survive the greatest tragedy. No illness, poverty or terror will make you doubt. Even if you die, you'll live."

There is more to life than being successful in work or performance. There is indestructible life from Christ that will carry you even if all else fails. Jesus doesn't turn you into Superman – He makes you indestructible.

# THERE YOU HAVE IT

*Jesus told him, "Go and
do likewise."*
Luke 10:37

▶ These words are the aftermath of the parable of the Good Samaritan. Jesus wanted to know which one – the priest, Levite, or the "objectionable" Samaritan – pleased God. When the Pharisees said, "The Samaritan, because he had compassion on the needy man," Jesus answered, "Good. There you have it. That's what God wants. Go and do likewise. It doesn't help to study the Word of God but not do what it says. God wants to see your compassion for others, not offerings. You'll do good to adhere to this."

We are often tempted to complicate God's will. It's not complicated. It's right before us. Be compassionate and please God.

Are you scared that people will misuse you if you're good and compassionate? Don't be scared. God's compassion and mercy have beautiful, loving and wise boundaries. Learn from Him how to do it. You'll enjoy it!

# RELAX, GUYS!

*"Even the very hairs of your head are all numbered. So don't be afraid; you are worth more than many sparrows."*
Matthew 10:30-31

▶ Jesus says, "Friends, you become so anxious about your lives and whether God really knows what is going on in and around you. It's unnecessary. Relax! If He finds it worthy to be involved in the lives of sparrows and insects and flowers, how much more will He not care for you? You are indeed the crown of creation. But still you cringe into a ball of stress about your own well-being, provision and care.

"You have no idea how intimately God is focused on you. Even the hairs of your head are numbered – can you believe it? Take a breath and let your heart relax in God's presence. Anxiety sucks the life out you."

Holy Father, my Father! Thank You for loving me. Thank You for knowing what is going on in my life. Thank You for embracing me. Thank You for not throwing me to the wolves, even when I tread on their hunting field. Amen.

# THE ROCKY PLACES OF THE HEART

*"Others, like seed sown on rocky places, hear the word and at once receive it with joy. But since they have no root, they last only a short time. When trouble or persecution comes because of the word, they quickly fall away."*

Mark 4:16-17

 A good example of a rocky heart is one that is focused on comfort. Everything must go according to plan and run smoothly. When people think that's what Jesus can offer them, they eagerly approach Him. But when the heat is one, they become despondent and walk away.

Do people promise you that Jesus will solve all your problems? You'll always have enough money, be healthy, have a good marriage, have healthy children, and get the job you want. So what are you going to do with Jesus when these things don't materialize? Many people lose all these things when they surrender their lives to Jesus – and then? The rocky hearts says, "Thank You, but no thank You." In this same way Jesus also lost most of His disciples in John 6.

Have you ever felt disappointed when Jesus didn't do what You asked of Him? I have. I had a rocky place in my heart and deserted Jesus, but He had mercy on me. What does your heart look like?

# "LET ME TAKE YOU TO THE FATHER"

*Jesus said to him,*
*"Follow Me."*
John 1:43

The Christian faith doesn't have inner peace and harmony with nature as its main goal. It has nothing to do with the realization of your inner self or the acquisition of some sort of cosmic illumination. It is concerned only about one cause: following Jesus. That is what the word *Christian* eminently implies.

Jesus walks in front and we follow carefully in His steps – nothing else. Of course Jesus doesn't just walk in any direction. He walks only in one direction – to the Father.

Everyone who follows Him will do what He does and reach the place where He is – the heart of the Father. When Jesus says, "Follow Me," He also says, "Let me take you to the Father."

Not following Jesus means never reaching the Father. You might feel that you're one with nature, but you'll never experience the joy of being one with the Father!

# PRUNING YIELDS A CROP

*"You are already clean because of
the word I have spoken to you."*
John 15:3

The words that Jesus spoke here are often compared to a sword coming from His mouth. This sword judges the world, but prunes the church. Jesus prunes all the things of the flesh and the things that are damaging to our lives, so that we can bear fruit that pleases God. To welcome Jesus' words into your life is to embrace God's blessing. To hunger after Jesus' words and to spend time listening to His words is to direct your life according to God's wisdom.

To do what Jesus says is to realize your purpose on earth. Nothing is more important than this. He prunes you and brings the best – God's life – to the fore.

Give Jesus free access to your heart. Allow Him to prune your life where He sees fit. It doesn't restrict you; in fact, it promotes God's life in you.

# THE LAMB IS ON THE THRONE

*"I know your deeds."*
Revelation 2:2

Jesus is depicted as the Righteous Judge of the nations who walks amid His church. He is always present. He is fully familiar with the lives of His disciples. He knows them. Nothing will happen to them without Him knowing about it. He is omnipresent for all eternity.

The idea is not one of Big Brother who spies on us, but rather of a loving Shepherd who cares for His sheep. Jesus' words in the Scripture verse are not a threat, but rather assurance of His involvement and insight. He says, "I'm in control. I reign. I know you. My eyes are on you. Just keep your eyes on Me."

An old hymn by Helen H. Lemmel proclaims: "Turn your eyes upon Jesus, look full in His wonderful face, and the things of earth will grow strangely dim, in the light of His glory and grace."

# THE LAST WORD

*"I have told you these things, so
that in Me you may have peace.
In this world you will have trouble.
But take heart! I have overcome
the world."*
John 16:33

"In this world you will have trouble." Not something
we really want to hear, but it's inextricably part of the
gospel. Where there is light, darkness seeks conflict.
Jesus doesn't say He will solve all our problems. On the
contrary, we're going to gain a few problems! But the
peace of Jesus doesn't come from the disappearance of
problems – it comes in the midst of problems.

Our peace is born from the fact that Jesus conquered
the grave and is the Righteous Judge of the nations. This
is so even if the world pushes you around and even kills
you. We are victorious with Jesus. We will have the last
word with Him.

Lord Jesus, please open my eyes to see You. Don't let my
circumstances and troubles let me lose sight of You. Help me
to be anchored in Your peace. Amen.

# I TOLD YOU SO

*"All the nations will be gathered before Him, and He will separate the people one from another as a shepherd separates the sheep from the goats."*
Matthew 25:32

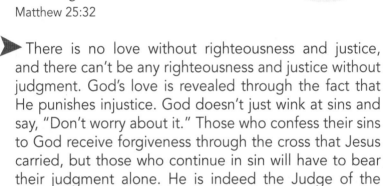

There is no love without righteousness and justice, and there can't be any righteousness and justice without judgment. God's love is revealed through the fact that He punishes injustice. God doesn't just wink at sins and say, "Don't worry about it." Those who confess their sins to God receive forgiveness through the cross that Jesus carried, but those who continue in sin will have to bear their judgment alone. He is indeed the Judge of the nations. Every knee will bow before Him.

"I've told you," Jesus says, "your peace lies in the fact that I have overcome this world and will demand a fair account before God. Be patient. It *will* happen."

Don't lose heart over the sins and destruction in the world. The end is near. God will separate His children from the disobedient and repay everyone according to what they've done.

# PURE HEARTS AND PIOUS APPEARANCES

*"Why do you entertain evil thoughts in your hearts?"*
Matthew 9:4

Jesus, the Righteous Judge, doesn't need cross examination and arguing to determine whether a person is guilty or not. On many occasions in the Bible He is described as the One with eyes like flames of fire before whom everything is exposed. Nothing is hidden from Him – especially not the depths of one's heart. He doesn't wonder or speculate or assume, and He doesn't make statements based on "the reasonable person."

He knows our plans, thoughts and pretenses. The question that Jesus asks here demands accountability. It's not just evil deeds that will be judged, but also the thoughts of the heart. Formalism will never please God. He asks for pure heart, not just pious faces.

Nothing is more private or more secret than a person's thoughts. To God, however, it's an open book. Protect your heart more than anything else, because from it comes life.

# OUR JOY
# AND PRIVILEGE

*"Be merciful, just as your Father is merciful."*
Luke 6:36

▶ Disciples of Jesus don't just do their best. They live through the Spirit of their Father and there is a big difference. The former is a human endeavor to excel, but the latter is a godly enabling. "Be like your Father. You were made in His image. His Spirit is in you." Disciples of Jesus do everything the Father does. They can, because He enables them.

Peter writes, "His divine power has given us everything we need for a godly life through our knowledge of Him who called us by His own glory and goodness" (2 Pet. 1:3).

Disciples' standards are no longer what the world says. Their goodness and mercy are not humanistic, but merciful like God. It's their privilege and joy.

If you're Jesus' disciple, born again through the Spirit of God, you won't be satisfied with anything less than what your Father says and does. Live from the wisdom of God!

# THAT'S HOW I DO IT

*Jesus said, "Take care
of My sheep."*
John 21:16

►Five powerful words from a significant, personal conversation between Jesus and Peter. "Peter, watch over My followers. There are many evil powers and forces that want to devour them, from inside the herd and from outside. Cherish them. Don't leave them to their own devices. You know firsthand how easy that can happen.

"Don't handle them too callously. Have compassion on them like I have compassion on them. Don't write them off when you feel disappointed in them. Give your life for them if you must. Protect them with your prayers, actions and words. I died for them, and for you. In the same way I restored you, you must restore them. Let your love for Me reflect in the way you care for them."

Don't become indifferent towards Jesus' disciples. Even if they're difficult, protect them and cherish them. This should be the case even when you're disappointed in them. That's how Jesus acts toward you.

# WORK WITH ME

*"Whoever is not with Me is against Me, and whoever does not gather with Me scatters."*
Matthew 12:30

"Whoever doesn't work with Me, works against Me. If your actions and words don't establish, comfort and encourage, then they upset, wound and discourage.

"Such a person does the opposite of what I do. Stop classifying people according to their church denomination. That doesn't bother Me. What is important is the answer to this question: Do you work *with* Me or *against* Me? Free yourself from the lie that only 'people who are like you' are connected to Me. You think that it's only 'your church's people' who follow Me. Don't be so shallow! Whoever is connected to Me does what I do. Don't oppose them."

Forgive me, Lord, for often opposing You in this way. I look at people and judge their works with immature, carnal beliefs. I want to side with those who work with You, regardless of their church denomination. Amen.

# THE GODLY FAMILY

*"Whoever does God's will is My brother and sister and mother."*
Mark 3:35

How do you know which people are truly part of God's family? It's easy – God's children are all apples that don't fall far from the Tree. Jesus (our eldest Brother) demonstrates this family trait best.

He said, "My food is to do the will of Him who sent Me (John 4:34). All God's children used to rebel against Him, but they don't do it anymore. The longing of their hearts now is only to do what the Father says. God's children want to do what He desires and accomplish His will. That's one thing all the members of God's family have in common."

Are you part of God's family? Do you do what He says? Don't "try" to do God's will. Surrender to His Spirit and it will happen automatically! Live a life worthy of your descent.

# AN ANOINTED MINISTRY

*"Now that I, your Lord and Teacher, have washed your feet, you also should wash one another's feet."*
John 13:14

To wash another's feet means to humbly serve others. We all want to serve, but Jesus puts *service* before *ministry*. In ministry your flesh can still feel superior, but in service the flesh is stripped. The washing of the guests' feet was reserved for the least important slaves. When Jesus took the washbasin and started serving His disciples, it caused an uproar.

Such service by an important person was regarded as a social embarrassment. But Jesus says, "If I, the Master, am willing to serve in this way, you must do the same. You're not more important. Find honor in this act." The right to minister often comes through service. As John C. Maxwell said: "People don't care how much you know until they know how much you care."

If you want to minister instead of serve, you will be driven by the flesh and not by God's Spirit. Do what Jesus says. Serve like Him, then you will also minister like Him.

# EXTRAORDINARILY ORDINARY

*"I have set you an example that you should do as I have done for you."*
John 13:15

➤ These comparative commands appear often in the New Testament: "If I … you should too." The reason for this is simple: A follower does what the leader does (otherwise they're not a follower).

Sometimes it feels like people think there are two types of Christians. One group consists of ordinary, everyday people, while the other is made up of "disciples of Jesus" – the more committed ones. That's a serious mistake. There is only one kind – followers of Christ. There are no generic types. You are either a follower or not.

If you say you are a follower of Jesus, you must do what He does. Followers don't live a life in contrast to the one they follow. They can't. They don't want to!

Fellow followers of our loving Christ mustn't fall for the world, and the argument of formalism that we are just mere humans. We are human, but the Spirit of Christ is in us. We don't have any other way to life.

# A BLESSING AND THE SON

*"Very truly I tell you, you will see 'heaven open, and the angels of God ascending and descending on' the Son of Man."*
John 1:51

The more you hear Jesus' words, the more it becomes evident that He wasn't just a great religious leader of His time. The heavens open up unto Him and the angels are His servants. He has complete access to the Father and is the center of God's attention.

While the Pharisees tried everything to dismiss Jesus as an outcast, God confirmed Him to be His unequivocal favorite. To be connected and committed to this Man is to receive God's blessing over your life. How the Father feels about His Son is also how He feels about everyone connected to the Son.

God's attention and His eyes are fixed on those who are dedicated to the Son. Pray more to see Jesus and less for blessings. The blessings of God will follow!

# FIT FOR SERVICE?

*"No one who puts a hand to the plow and looks back is fit for service in the kingdom of God."*
Luke 9:62

There is something else that distracts this plower. It's interesting to note that he keeps looking back. Whatever it is, it's competing with the work he is doing. Jesus says, "If you side with God and His will but still regard worldly things as competition, you're not yet ready for God's kingdom.

"If the world still allures you to plow while looking back all the time, you're not convinced that the world has nothing to offer you. You're not convinced of God's kingdom. Your hands are on the plow, but your heart is elsewhere. If your heart finds reason to be divided and not focused on God alone, you're not fit for God's work."

God does not only long after undivided hearts, He demands it. Examine your heart. Where do you stand? Are you almost convinced that the world has nothing to offer? Then you're not convinced at all that Jesus is our only Source.

# EXTRAORDINARY ACTION

*"Come, follow Me," Jesus said, "and I will send you out to fish for people."*
Mark 1:17

▶ Fishing was the language of Peter and Andrew's hearts. They knew all the ins and outs of fishing and were good enough to make a living from it. Jesus used the vocabulary from their world to call them as disciples. He says, "You are good at what you do. Come, follow Me, and I will make you even better – greater catches will follow!"

What defines your world? A fitter and turner? A doctor? A policeman? Jesus acknowledges your profession and your gifts. He tells you, "You have no idea what I can do through and with you. I can take you to heights you never thought possible. Follow in My steps and become part of the action of God's kingdom!"

Peter and Andrew would never have thought that they would become part of God's actions and plans. Maybe you can also not imagine this. You don't have to – just follow Jesus …

# MORE IMPORTANT THAN FOOD

*"It is written: 'Man shall not live on bread alone, but on every word that comes from the mouth of God.'"*
Matthew 4:4

▶ This was Jesus' answer to Satan's temptation to use God for His own personal gain. Jesus said, "Your slyness is obvious. Since when do people flourish when they get everything they want? That's a lie.

"People's happiness and joy in life are not determined by getting what they want or desire or even need, but by applying the truth of God – everything God says is true, and gives life.

"It fulfills even the depths of the soul. To adhere to the Word of God is to be nourished even more than food can nourish the body. Every time a person exchanges God's word for what people offer, they embrace death."

God is not a capitalist, socialist or communist. Worldly systems gladly replace the Word of God and truth with their own philosophies. Behind this hides the tempter with the same lies he used to tempt Jesus.

# UNNECESSARY!
# IMPOSSIBLE!

*"You should not be surprised at My saying, 'You must be born again.'"*
John 3:7

A well-read religious leader visited Jesus to discuss the kingdom of God. Jesus surprised him by saying that if a person is not born again, they will never see or enter into the kingdom of God. The "born-again" story sounded a bit much to the man. "Don't look so surprised," Jesus said, "you've entered into this world by being born. Likewise, you must enter God's kingdom by being born again.

"Your first birth was a physical one. Your second will be a spiritual one through God's Spirit. If God doesn't allow you to be born into His kingdom, you'll never experience it. And the only way to experience this birth is through Me."

If you don't need Jesus, you'll never experience being born again and you'll never enter into God's kingdom. Then you are hopelessly lost.

# HARVEST TIME

*"Don't you have a saying, 'It's still four months until harvest'? I tell you, open your eyes and look at the fields! They are ripe for harvest."*
John 4:35

Harvest time in my little town is a big event and very exciting. From all over tractors with heavily loaded carriages of grapes wind their way to the cellars, bringing in the harvest. People sometimes work straight through the night to harvest the grapes and load them so that nothing goes to waste.

Jesus looks at His people and says, "It's harvest time on the farm!" People hunger for salvation and healing and the message of God's wonderful answer is right there.

It's time to bring in the heavenly harvest. People are tired of religion that doesn't satisfy their hunger and thirst. They long for God's touch and true ministry.

When we see what God sees, it awakens something deep in our hearts to help bring in the harvest. That's the secret. Never assume that you know or that you can see.

# APRIL

# BLISSFULLY SATISFIED

*"Blessed are those who hunger and thirst for righteousness, for they will be filled."*
Matthew 5:6

One can long after many things, even good things, but not necessarily after what is right in God's eyes. One can satisfy one's desires with what the world has to offer, but the hunger will quickly return.

There is a hunger that can truly be satisfied and that is a hunger after righteousness. When the Bible talks about righteousness, it talks about being made right with God. Jesus says we can be "right" with God. We can be reconciled with Him and do what is right in His eyes. It's possible because God makes it possible. The question is never if God *will* do something, but rather if we really want it.

Which things in your life prevent you from longing after righteousness? Is it ambition, lust, money? Whatever it is, it's robbing you of true fulfillment and power. Don't allow it to continue.

# THE TRUE GOSPEL

*"Very truly I tell you, no one can see the kingdom of God unless they are born again."*
John 3:3

▶ For many years people strongly opposed the preaching of being born again. My own parents were censured and asked to leave the church because of it. But no one can stop the work of the Spirit! That same church now fearlessly preaches the words of Jesus. Unless you are born again it is impossible to enter or see the kingdom of God.

In this way Jesus is also saying, "The time is coming when anyone who kills you will think they are offering a service to God" (John 16:2). The devil has his own version of the gospel and preaches it fervently even from the pulpit. But Jesus' words are the only ones that can bring life and salvation.

Any form of the gospel in conflict with that of Jesus is a demonic gospel. It's artfully constructed to keep people from entering God's kingdom. Keep to the original – that's the only truth!

# A GREAT PRIVILEGE

*"No one can enter the kingdom of God unless they are born of water and the Spirit. Flesh gives birth to flesh, but the Spirit gives birth to spirit."*
John 3:5-6

"Flesh gives birth to flesh." Nothing that comes from human nature can please God, but what is born from the Spirit is spirit. This is where the godly secret lies. The gospel of Jesus is not only Good News, but also the power of God that brings salvation to everyone who believes (see Rom. 1:16).

That's the greatest miracle of all! Without it no one will be part of God's family. God's children aren't just adopted. We are born into His family by faith in Jesus Christ. We're all His children. We take after our Father; we do what our Father does and sit with Him on the throne. We rule over the works of Satan.

Don't be content with a mere dedicated religious life. It's not enough. Be born again. It's the beginning of the greatest adventure of your life!

# GOD'S GLORY SHINES THROUGH

*"Neither this man nor his parents sinned," said Jesus, "but this happened so that the works of God might be displayed in him."*
John 9:3

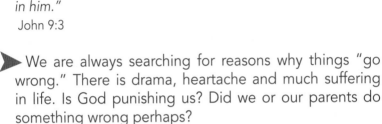

We are always searching for reasons why things "go wrong." There is drama, heartache and much suffering in life. Is God punishing us? Did we or our parents do something wrong perhaps?

The truth is that most of these things have to do with the decay and brokenness in the world we live in. The result of sin in humans' lives and on this earth is staggering. It causes widespread grief in all areas of life.

Jesus says, "This man is suffering because the world is broken. But life and glory will become evident when He gives him life. God's plans and intentions with man will become clearly evident."

Father, reveal Your glory in me. Let my whole life, especially my brokenness, become a platform for Your life and power so that others can see what You have planned for us. Amen.

# YOU CHOOSE;
# I REIGN

*"Whoever wants to be My disciple must deny themselves and take up their cross daily and follow Me."*
Luke 9:23

Jesus' message is simple: "If you want to follow Me, I'm the Lord – not you. You have many dreams and plans, opinions and ideas, beliefs and observations – more than you can think. Tie it all together and give it to Me. If you follow Me – if I'm your Lord – you have to learn from Me and not think you know all the answers.

"I will teach you what is right and true. I will reveal God to you. I will teach you about people and especially about yourself. If you follow Me, it's non-negotiable – you'll have to do exactly as I say. Remember, I'm the Way – not your fears or desires or preferences."

Without this mindset it's impossible to follow Jesus. Without it, at the most you'll be a fellow traveler, walking with the Lord when it pleases you. It was such people who crucified Jesus.

# CHOOSE JESUS' YOKE

*"Take My yoke upon you and learn from Me, for I am gentle and humble in heart, and you will find rest for your souls."*
Matthew 11:29

Two things stand out here. Firstly, sin and formalism are heavy, ruthless burdens (read Matt. 11). They exhaust people and crush them to the ground. Secondly, Jesus also offers a yoke – He is not unyoked.

Discipleship has demands, but these demands lead to life. Jesus' yoke is made up of the grace and compassion of God. This yoke does not destroy. It does not exhaust. It offers life and rest for the soul. Jesus is not a slave driver. He is humble and gentle. He is 100 percent in line with the will of the Father. His demands lead to salvation, reconciliation, healing and liberation.

Jesus doesn't throw His yoke on you. It's your responsibility to take it upon yourself. Is the yoke you carry that of Jesus? Test it: does it bring rest for your soul or does it make you restless and uneasy?

# FORGIVE WILLINGLY

*"I tell you, her many sins have been forgiven – as her great love has shown. But whoever has been forgiven little loves little."*
Luke 7:47

These words mean so much to me. The principle of love is to realize what God has done for me. When I understand how God has forgiven me for so many things and loves me unconditionally and indescribably, my heart swells with love, appreciation and worship for Him.

It also unlocks my heart to love and forgive others like I've never been able to. Ignorance wraps me in arrogance, thinking that people don't deserve my forgiveness and love. Conversely, no one who understands God's love and forgiveness will be conditional with their love. Read Matthew 18 and hear what God is saying to you.

Father, reveal Your love to me so that my whole life is illuminated by it. Open my eyes to understand Your love so that I too can love unconditionally. Amen.

# SERVING IN
# THE PIT

*"If the blind lead the blind, both will
fall into a pit."*
Matthew 15:14

Logical? Perhaps, but not obviously so. There are many blind people presenting themselves as leaders, guiding other blind people without others becoming suspicious. Jesus regards anyone who doesn't acknowledge Him for who He is and who shows no insight into the kingdom of God as blind.

Religion produces many such blind people. This often happens with people who have theological schooling, but their eyes have not been opened by Jesus. The fruits of their service are the pit. Not only do they fall into the pit of ignorance and sin themselves, but they also guide others to follow them into darkness. As blind leaders, they act brave and take the lead, but they're still blind and unable to see the truth of God.

How sad that many religious leaders are in fact spiritually blind! But it's a greater tragedy when I think that I can see, and can't. Please open my eyes to see Jesus! Amen.

# THE GREATEST DECLARATION OF LOVE

*"As the Father has loved Me, so have I loved you. Now remain in My love."*
John 15:9

These words are indeed the greatest love declaration of all time! To understand how much Jesus loves you, you have to understand how much the Father loves the Son. There is no greater love than this. The Father absolutely adores His Son!

God will use every opportunity to declare and visibly demonstrate His love towards Jesus. "This is My Son, whom I love; with Him I am well pleased," says the Father in Matthew 3:17. This statement is repeated several times in the New Testament. It is a completely selfless, unashamed love. It is exactly how Jesus feels about you.

"This is My beloved brother and sister; with them I am well pleased," says Jesus. That's what He is saying about you. Stronger fellowship and dedication you won't find anywhere.

Lord Jesus, I can think of a thousand reasons why I don't qualify for Your love, but none of them are valid. You love me. You gave Yourself for me. I worship You! Amen.

# REFLECT THE TRUTH

*"What about you?" Jesus asked.*
*"Who do you say I am?"*
Matthew 16:15

▶ This is the great eternal question. It resounds throughout the ages and confronts us every day. Is Jesus who He said He is, and can others see the answer to this question through your life?

The world is divided up into two parts. The one part says "no" and the other group says "yes." Among those who say yes, there is a second confrontation: "Show me how you live so that I can see if your answer is true." It's easy to say, "Yes, Jesus is the Son of the Living God," but then live as if this is not true. Such witnessing has no value. Those who truly believe that He is the Alpha and Omega, the King of kings, live a life reflecting this truth in practical ways.

If Jesus is your Lord, let it be evident that He is Lord and not you. While the world might regard your lifestyle as ludicrous, they will secretly admire the integrity of your testimony. This glorifies God.

# WHEN HATE BECOMES HONOR

*"If the world hates you, keep in mind that it hated Me first."*
John 15:18

No one is particularly fond of rejection and hatred from others. It's not romantic or heroic. It's lonely and hurtful. Jesus says, "Regard yourselves as fortunate because you are receiving the same treatment from the world that I endured.

"It's their way of acknowledging that you belong to Me. If you were part of them, they wouldn't treat you this way. You're citizens of the light. Darkness hates light. Don't turn to the world to heal your hurts, you'll only get wounded again. Turn to Me for healing and comfort. My Father will accept you and clothe you with glory. To the world you may be an embarrassment, but to God your life will reflect honor!"

To be associated with Jesus is the greatest honor. Don't exchange this for the cheap and erratic recognition of the world.

# BE IN AGREEMENT

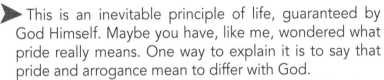

*"I tell you that this man, rather than the other, went home justified before God. For all those who exalt themselves will be humbled, and those who humble themselves will be exalted."*
Luke 18:14

This is an inevitable principle of life, guaranteed by God Himself. Maybe you have, like me, wondered what pride really means. One way to explain it is to say that pride and arrogance mean to differ with God.

True humility is to be in agreement with God. Everyone who differs with God walks in pride in that specific area. Such a person will always land themselves in trouble. God knows what He's talking about, even if it makes no sense to you. Every person who undauntingly agrees with Him will be declared pure and holy.

God opposes the proud, but gives grace to the humble (see James 4:6). The more our lives are in agreement with God; the more we will be restored.

In which areas do you differ from God? Is it in your resentment for your enemy or in placing more worth in the people around you? Do you acknowledge your sin and impurity? Don't allow pride to rob you of God's blessings!

# UNDERSTANDING HEAVENLY THINGS

*"I have spoken to you of earthly things and you do not believe; how then will you believe if I speak of heavenly things?"*
John 3:12

The inability of the human flesh to understand the things of God is absolutely staggering. Jesus' frustration with the flesh is evident from His words, "Why is My language not clear to you? Because you are unable to hear what I say" (John 8:43). Years later Paul wrote: "The person without the Spirit does not accept the things that come from the Spirit of God but considers them foolishness, and cannot understand them because they are discerned only through the Spirit" (1 Cor. 2:14).

That is why it is necessary to be born again, and why formalism stands in such stark contrast to God. That is why Jesus offers a different yoke, and why we need the Spirit of God – to open our eyes!

Jesus is the only way to end the blindness of the flesh. In Him we not only share in God's life, but also *understand* His life.

# NOTHING WITHOUT JESUS

*"I am the vine; you are the branches. If you remain in Me and I in you, you will bear much fruit; apart from Me you can do nothing."*
John 15:5

Jesus is the life of the believer. He is the center of God's church. From Him flows godly life and abundance to those who are committed to Him. When people or the church turn to other things, their lives begin to wither. Unfortunately this happens often.

When congregations long for revival and restoration they turn to trendy programs and new and contemporary methods to bring about change. There's nothing wrong with that, but if it becomes the main aim, then it is wrong. When they should turn to Jesus, people turn to other people and programs. Instead of being restored, they fall further into destruction. However, to the person longing for unity with Christ, love and glory awaits.

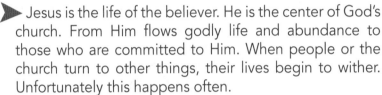

Turn back to Jesus. Always turn back to Him. His character, person and ministry is the secret to making everything good. Find your answers in Him.

# NO GREATER LOVE

*"For God so loved the world that He gave His one and only Son, that whoever believes in Him shall not perish but have eternal life."*
John 3:16

Although we resist God's love, it's breathtaking to hear that He still loves us. Something within us calls out to it. We don't want to accept His love because we don't want to accept His rule, but we know that His love is the only thing that can heal the wounds of our souls.

Love gives; it doesn't take back. God gave His Son. What makes this gift so astonishing is that we don't deserve it at all! We deserve judgment, not love and grace. Still God gives it to us. Greater love no one can find. The question is not how unworthy we are of receiving this love, but rather what we do with it.

Think about it. What do you do with the love God shows you? Do you embrace it, or push it away? Only a fool will continue to resist. Embrace love and life!

# THE APPLE OF HIS EYE

*"If anyone gives even a cup of cold water to one of these little ones who is My disciple, truly I tell you, that person will certainly not lose their reward."*
Matthew 10:42

▶ When Jesus said that He loves His disciples in the same way the Father loves Him, He meant every word. Nothing would happen to His disciples without Him knowing about it.

Any good deed for His disciples because they follow Him will be rewarded by Jesus Himself. The opposite is, of course, also true. Any damage or hurt done to someone because they follow Jesus will be punished by Him. Jesus' eyes are on His disciples – day and night – because He loves them. Touch them and you touch Him. Jesus' disciples are the apple of His eye. He confirms this with His words "truly I tell you."

Jesus' disciples might seem simple to the world, but in God's eyes they're precious beyond words. There is a reward from God for the way we treat His children.

# IMPORTANT INFORMATION

*"You are the light of the world.*
*A town built on a hill*
*cannot be hidden."*
Matthew 5:14

People who are not committed to Jesus cannot see or experience Him. The only contact they have with Jesus is His life and truth that shine through His followers.

If you are a follower of Jesus, this is very important information! It means that your life is not "ordinary" anymore. It becomes the showcase for the gospel. It's not your infallibility or faultlessness that is the light, but rather your reaction towards God's truth amid your faults and immaturity. It's God's truth in you that shows other people that there is hope, salvation and life in Jesus.

You don't have to pretend. Be sincere and genuine before God and people.

People aren't moved by the masks that people wear, but rather by sincerity and truth. Don't be scared to be genuine. Be vulnerable in God's truth – it brings godly relief!

# THE WEIGHT OF YOUR WORDS

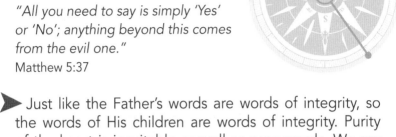

*"All you need to say is simply 'Yes' or 'No'; anything beyond this comes from the evil one."*
Matthew 5:37

▶ Just like the Father's words are words of integrity, so the words of His children are words of integrity. Purity of the heart is inevitable as well as pure words. We say what we mean and we mean what we say. It cannot be anything else. If David prayed, "May these words of my mouth and this meditation of my heart be pleasing in Your sight, Lord, my Rock and my Redeemer" (Ps. 19:14), this is exactly what he's talking about.

We know that we stand before a living God who sees everything and to whom we must give account for everything we say and do. Jesus explains: "By your words you will be acquitted, and by your words you will be condemned" (Matt. 12:37).

May the salvation and purity of God also reflect through your words. May the integrity of your words confirm your commitment to Jesus. Anything besides this comes from the evil one.

# THE CRUMBS

*"When you pray, go into your
room, close the door and pray
to your Father, who is unseen.
Then your Father, who sees what
is done in secret, will reward you."*
Matthew 6:6

A relationship with God is not about show and public display. When you struggle with feelings of inferiority, you often try to compensate for it in other ways. Sometimes it's through spiritual pretense. Resist it at all costs. Enjoy God without window dressing. Let your relationship with Him become the most important thing in your life – don't just love Him for what you can get out of Him.

Love God for who He is. Everything you need will flow from this relationship – healing, fulfillment, salvation. Those who are satisfied with a relationship for the show must be satisfied with the crumbs. God's love inspires us to greater things than just crumbs. He says, "I'm First Prize! Get to know Me – wonderful surprises await you."

Father, many times my heart deceives me. Help me to get to know Your purity and sincerity. Open my eyes to see and experience You. Fill my life with You. Amen.

# A MERE SHEPHERD BOY

*"Whoever can be trusted with very little can also be trusted with much, and whoever is dishonest with very little will also be dishonest with much."*
Luke 16:10

▶ Years ago a preacher said, "God is not interested in your comfort, He is interested in your character." It has stuck with me ever since. Sometimes our search for God is predominantly experience driven. We measure our spiritual growth and depth against our experiences of spirituality. God doesn't.

Obedience to Jesus produces godly character that is indisputable in any place on earth. Our spirituality and depth are measured against the presence of Christ's character in our lives. The more spiritual and mature we are, the more we'll become like Jesus in character. Things like reliability and honesty come from deep inside the heart and really reflect the truth of God.

It's not the "big things" that determine greatness, but rather how much we can be trusted with the small things.

## Application

Resist the world's definition of greatness. David didn't become king because he was the cleverest and strongest, but because he was the most faithful, a mere shepherd boy.

# SIGNS AND WONDERS

*"Unless you people see signs and wonders," Jesus told him, "you will never believe."*
John 4:48

This statement was an accusation, not a declaration about the importance of signs and wonders. Jesus says, "You believe in Me because I do what you want, not because of who I am. As long as I perform miracles and make your lives easier, you love Me. But if I demand something from you because I'm the Lord, you want nothing to do with Me. Your faith is superficial and insufficient and doesn't please God."

People who follow Jesus because of the excitement of experiences and events will quickly stop following Him when emotions diminish – and they will! The test is this: Is Jesus who He said He is, even if He doesn't do what you want?

You will have to pass this test many times if you want to succeed in growing in your relationship with God. What will you do when the great experiences dry up and Jesus doesn't answer your prayers? Will you still follow Him?

# PETER'S LESSON

*Jesus answered, "If I want him to remain alive until I return, what is that to you? You must follow Me."*
John 21:22

When Jesus told Peter how he was going to die he wanted to know, "And what about John? What's going to happen to him? Will he get special treatment as the dearly loved disciple?" Jesus' answer is frank: "Peter, My actions and relationship with other people have nothing to do with you. Make sure *your* life is pleasing and pure before God. Stick to your own business. What I decide to do in the lives of others doesn't concern you."

Peter was reprimanded in the process. Are we the same? "Lord, but what about so-and-so …?" We'd do well to learn this lesson from Peter's life!

Keep your eyes on Jesus and forget about the people around you. They're responsible for their own lives. Make sure you are pure before God, regardless of what anyone else does.

# IF I HAD ONLY KNOWN ...

*"If you knew the gift of God and who it is that asks you for a drink, you would have asked Him and He would have given you living water."*
John 4:10

"If you had known whom you were dealing with, this conversation would've gone differently." I've thought about this a lot when I think back on situations and moments in my life. If I've known then that Jesus was with me and that He even had a plan with whatever happened to me, I would've reacted differently. I know this now. When you discover this, it unlocks your heart and all of a sudden you understand. It's so healing! It even influences how and what you pray.

Jesus is with you and me in everything. He knows what we don't know yet. If we understand this, everything changes. Be on the look-out for this today.

Lord Jesus, I've asked so many times before, but I'm asking again, please open my eyes to really see You! May I know in every situation, including in crises, that You are with me. Amen.

# GOD'S JUDGMENT

*"Very truly I tell you, whoever hears My word and believes Him who sent Me has eternal life and will not be judged but has crossed over from death to life."*
John 5:24

God's judgment is very real. It's an unpopular subject for people, but not for God. True love and righteousness require judgment over sins and unrighteousness. God is love and truly pure, therefore He will always judge impurity. It's inevitable. If you accept God's authority, you will be exempt from judgment, because Jesus has been judged in your place.

Jesus says, "I assure you: whoever submits to God is free from being judged. I'll carry it for you. You'll be free from judgment and also receive the privilege of getting to know God. That's true life."

There is no such thing as a judgment-free gospel. Either we carry it, or Jesus does, but it's always there. "Therefore, there is now no condemnation for those who are in Christ Jesus" (Rom. 8:1).

# RESTORED AND REVIVED

*"I have food to eat that you know nothing about. My food is, "said Jesus, "to do the will of Him who sent me and to finish His work."*
John 4:32, 34

There is a secret of being fulfilled that belongs only to Jesus and His followers, namely doing the will of the Father. We don't understand why we are put on earth, what our purpose is or where we're heading, until we do what God wants us to.

Then our eyes are opened and we start to understand the reason behind it all. Then we understand what the highest ambition on earth is. Our whole existence as humans is defined when we do what He says.

Like food fills a hungry person and brings them comfort, likewise obedience to God fulfills the soul.

Our souls were hungry and without purpose because of our disobedience to God. We don't have to dwell in the desert any longer. Feed your soul by being obedient to the One who loves you.

# THE RIGHTEOUS JUDGE

*"Do not judge, or you too will be judged."*
Matthew 7:1

There is a difference between discernment and judgment. To discern means to be able to see the difference between the works of the flesh and the works of God. It's vitally important to be able to discern! To judge means to take the place of God as Righteous Judge – a position that belongs to Him alone.

Such a person will have to give account for his or her arrogance and rebellion. There is only One who can and is allowed to judge. If you're wondering if your efforts to discern are not judgmental, ask yourself this question: Do I more often discern the works of the flesh in other people's lives or more often in my own heart? Don't try to take Jesus' place as Judge – it will land you in the dock.

Start first with your own heart. Don't tolerate any impurity of thought, character or reaction in your life. Don't say anything about someone else while you're impure before God.

# "SAFE" SINS?

*"See, you are well again. Stop sinning or something worse may happen to you."*
John 5:14

It doesn't matter how you look at it – sin destroys. While not all sickness and illness are directly linked to sin, sin is the single main cause of death and destruction on earth. Without it we wouldn't have known about wounds and destruction.

No one can live in sin and escape unharmed. Sins cause wounds – always. Not only does sin eventually lead to judgment, but sin also leads its followers down a road of drama and trauma that causes immense damage. This is evident in the suffering that Jesus had to endure to free us from it. This should not be taken lightly, and Jesus' warning should not be ignored.

There is no safe way to deal with sin. Satan may let the world believe in "safe sins," but that's a lie – typical to his nature. Believe in Jesus and be set free!

# AN AGENDA WITH ETERNAL VALUE

*"Let us go somewhere else – to the nearby villages – so I can preach there also. That is why I have come."*
Mark 1:38

As someone who is in ministry myself, it is striking that Jesus was not "ministry orientated," but "people orientated." Jesus didn't focus on a "big ministry," but rather on ensuring that as many people as possible should hear His message. His own interests and importance didn't feature on the agenda; instead, the salvation and deliverance of all people were most important.

That was the mission He was sent on by God. This makes you seriously consider your own agenda and mission. What is my own focus? Is it the same as Jesus? Am I faithful to what God has called me to, or am I on a sidetrack of "good things" instead of "God things"? Weigh your life and decide for yourself.

Don't exchange your life for "good things." Stay vigilant and focused on God's agenda. It's the only agenda with eternal value.

# A GODLY MANDATE

*"The work of God is this: to believe in the One He has sent."*
John 6:29

What does God want from us? It's a question many people ask. Jesus answered this question already. God asks that we believe that Jesus is who He said He is and that we obey Him. Paul wrote, "God is faithful, who has called you into fellowship with His Son, Jesus Christ our Lord" (1 Cor. 1:9).

From this calling comes our ministry and service to others. Paul again explains, "All this is from God, who reconciled us to Himself through Christ and gave us the ministry of reconciliation" (2 Cor. 5:18). Here God answers three of our most important questions: What does God require from me? What is my calling? What is my ministry?

If we embrace and understand these three truths our lives will suddenly obtain new meaning. We are vocation-oriented beings! No one in God's kingdom is without a purpose and we're all important. We live with a divine mandate.

# TRUE AND FALSE CONVERSIONS

*"Repent, for the kingdom of heaven has come near."*
Matthew 4:17

▶ Being converted doesn't only mean to "turn away from." It also means to "turn towards." God appeals to us to turn our backs on sin and turn to Him. People try to turn away from sin by turning to "a better life." That won't work! Salvation and deliverance can only be found in God.

Jesus says, "People, God is with you. He reigns. Turn to Him. *He* will heal and save you. Don't think you can save yourself from sin. You can't. Turn to God. Acknowledge Him. Confess that He is true and pure. Plead with Him to save you. That's exactly what He wants to do for you!"

To be converted doesn't mean to stop sinning. It means first of all to accept God's authority. Then it brings deliverance from sin. God's rule – His kingdom – is the answer we're longing for.

# MAY

# A VALUABLE LESSON

*"By Myself I can do nothing; I judge only as I hear, and My judgment is just, for I seek not to please Myself but Him who sent Me."*
John 5:30

Jesus brought this principle repeatedly under the attention of the disciples (and the Pharisees). He is 100 percent under the authority of the Father, and He does nothing without His approval. That was the foundation of His authority.

It means: If the Son of God submits to the Father in everything, how much more must His followers not do this? If this was the principle of Jesus' ministry on earth, how much more must this not be the principle by which we live? That's the important message. We have no authority unless we stand completely under the rule of God and do what He asks of us.

If Jesus lives in you through the Holy Spirit, it's absolutely possible to live like Him. That's what it means to live through the Spirit. Allow Jesus to be King in your life.

# MORE THAN A PLASTER

*"It is not the healthy who need a doctor, but the sick."*
Luke 5:31

To know your needs is often the biggest breakthrough in getting the right treatment. Someone who doesn't know that they need a doctor won't go looking for one. There are many people walking around with deadly diseases without even knowing it. Then there are those who know, but carry on casually. The third group realizes they're sick and urgently seek help.

Sin and being lost work the same way. Jesus is the ultimate Doctor of the soul. Those who know that they're lost in their own sins can call on Him to heal them. If complete healing of the soul is possible, why would one not seize this opportunity?

The Holy Spirit can make a very accurate diagnosis of the heart. Jesus doesn't just cover wounds with a plaster. Be open and reach out to Jesus. He is right by your side!

# A LIGHT IN THE TUNNEL

*"I have come into the world as a light, so that no one who believes in Me should stay in darkness."*
John 12:46

▶ The Bible is clear about this. God doesn't want anyone to be lost. He doesn't want anyone to continue living with cancer in their soul. He doesn't want anyone to live in darkness.

God's salvation and light are available to everyone, but it's not necessarily what everyone wants. Many people *want* to live in darkness and disaster (however strange that may seem). The choice remains yours. Those who long for the light of Christ receive it in great glory and experience how the darkness is driven from their lives. Those with pure hearts become even more pure. But those who want to stay in darkness fall even deeper into destruction.

Lord Jesus, Light of God, light up every corner of my life with Your truth and life. May darkness find no hiding place in my heart. Amen.

# "HOW CAN I DO THIS, LORD?"

*"Therefore I tell you, do not worry about your life, what you will eat or drink; or about your body, what you will wear. Is not life more than food, and the body more than clothes?"*
Matthew 6:25

What a question! The spontaneous answer to this question could be, "Never! Food and clothes are what it is all about!" A person's approach to life can easily become a mere survival philosophy of keeping your head above water or a superficial life focused only on comfort and material things. Could there be something more to life?

Jesus says so: "The greatest fulfillment and purpose of life is to do what God wants. Nothing is greater than this." Jesus taught His disciples that people who live to please God and to do what He says, will never fall into the pit of worry and concern about provision. God will handle this. Just set your focus on the right things.

Obedience to God in everything doesn't guarantee wealth, but God promises provision in all circumstances. Keep your eyes on Jesus and experience how He will supernaturally care for you.

# BECAUSE HE LIVES

*"Therefore do not worry about tomorrow, for tomorrow will worry about itself. Each day has enough trouble of its own."*
Matthew 6:34

Jesus is *not* saying here that we should sit and do Bible study the whole day and not work. That's not true! Strive to work with your hands, but put your life focus on being obedient to God and not worrying about survival.

Jesus doesn't preach a gospel that says we will never have sorrow or trouble. What He *is* saying is that we don't need to cross each bridge before we get to it, but rather focus on what is in front of us. We deal with our concerns in our daily walk with Him, and He resolves our fears because He is in control. He cares for us.

In 1 Peter 5:7 the Bible tells us: "Cast all your anxiety on Him because He cares for you." Trust God with your problems. Let worry be replaced by the supremacy of Jesus.

# "WHAT DO YOU NEED?"

*"What do you want Me to do for you?" Jesus asked.*
Mark 10:36

This is a very specific question, but the answer reveals our focus. There are many things we can ask of Jesus, but it's not necessarily the best things. Two of Jesus' disciples asked to be seated in positions of honor around His throne. They could've asked for pure hearts, forgiving spirits, reconciliation, a special revelation of the Father, but they chose status and self glory.

Interesting! Jesus rejected their request. The Father will honor people. If they've asked to know the will of the Father and the wisdom to do it, they would've automatically qualified for seats of honor.

Don't just ask for good things, ask for the best! Allow the Holy Spirit to help you. If you do this, you'll experience amazing answers to prayer.

# AMIDST CRISES

*Jesus Himself stood among them
and said, "Peace be with you."*
Luke 24:36

▶ Peace is not just a blissful feeling stripped of worries and tension. It's much more! Peace is the presence of God's rule. Where God reigns, there is peace. It's a state of respect for and worship of God. Jesus is the King of the kingdom. Wherever He goes He brings the rule of God. He brings God's peace. That's why He is the Great Peacemaker.

People can experience the control and presence of God and rest in His peace amidst great crises. Peace is more than a feeling. It's God's reality. Paul talks about the peace "which transcends all understanding" (see Phil. 4:7). That's God's peace.

If peace eludes you, pray this prayer: "Lord, in which things am I still being disobedient?" and "Lord, show me where You are in this situation." Search for God's authority in your life.

# JESUS – THE POWER OF OUR LIVES

*"You will receive power when the Holy Spirit comes on you; and you will be My witnesses in Jerusalem, and in all Judea and Samaria, and to the ends of the earth."*
Acts 1:8

An outstanding characteristic of the ministry of the Holy Spirit is the absolute focus on Jesus. He reminds the disciples about what Jesus had said and done; He revealed Jesus' power and enabled the disciples to be witnesses of His glory.

The world is evil, and we need godly power to witness for Jesus. This requires courage and zeal. It requires God. The Holy Spirit is the godly fire burning in the lives of His disciples – which urges and inspires them to witness about the Alpha and Omega, the Beginning and the End. Disciples with the power of the Holy Spirit in them can't keep Jesus to themselves.

Is your testimony weak, intimidated, or broken? You need the power of the Holy Spirit. Read Acts 2 and 4. Ask the Father to strengthen you. Keep on asking and seeking until you find it.

# PLAN YOUR FUTURE

*"Blessed are the merciful, for they will be shown mercy."*
Matthew 5:7

We reap what we sow. We desperately want to sow money and reap bagfuls of it, but God's focus is elsewhere. His focus is on sowing what is right and godly. Sow what is important to Him and you'll reap God's ministry.

If you sow kindness, you'll not only reap kindness from other people, but also rich compassion, mercy and favor from God. Is God real to you? Then sow His words. Never tire of doing this, because at the right time you will reap your reward that God has promised. As sure as God lives, it will happen. The opposite is also true. Sow harshness and mercilessness and you'll receive it back twofold. God guarantees it.

Don't wander away from God. He will not be mocked. That which a person sows, they will reap. Plan your future together with Jesus. Every decision and action counts!

# GOD'S MEASURE

*"I tell you that anyone who is angry with a brother or sister will be subject to judgment."*
Matthew 5:22

Remember how we've said that God's system is different from that of the world? This is an excellent example. Jesus says, "Don't think that if you haven't slept around with other people you haven't committed adultery. If you desire someone with lustful eyes, you've been adulterous. Don't think that if you haven't physically killed someone, you haven't murdered. If you've cut someone out in anger and ruined the relationship, you've committed murder.

"That is God's truth. Relationships are as valuable as the people they consist of. To destroy relationships is as good as destroying a person." Is this a tough measure? It's the true measure. That's why we need Jesus to cleanse our hearts.

When we understand God's value system, our needs increase from purity to sanctification. Don't be satisfied with the world's values. Let Jesus teach you.

# A LOW-INCOME INVESTMENT

*"Do not store up for yourselves treasures on earth, where moths and vermin destroy, and where thieves break in and steal."*
Matthew 6:19

This is another worldly value that fails! We can work for years and spend incalculable energy storing up treasures on earth. It's silly. Not only can these treasures get damaged or stolen, but they're also quite worthless.

Money can't buy loving relationships. Money has no eternal value and doesn't provide security. Oftentimes it actually increases our lack of peace and joy and makes us think that we don't need God. Why would we put such a high premium on an inadequate and low income investment? If Jesus really knows what He's talking about, then let it be evident through your value system. Your treasure will show the world your heart.

Although financial institutions don't regard things of eternal value as important, don't be fooled. God knows what He's talking about.

# SIGNIFICANT DIVIDENDS

*"Store up for yourselves treasures in heaven, where moths and vermin do not destroy, and where thieves do not break in and steal."*
Matthew 6:20

▶ This is God's alternative. Heavenly treasures cannot become obsolete, get damaged or be stolen. It holds the promise of loving, fulfilling relationships and eternal love and joy. (It's a dark day when you think that earthly treasures can establish all of that.)

In the same way it requires dedication and hard work to collect treasures on earth, it takes zeal and dedication to collect heavenly treasures. It's a lifestyle of obedience to Christ and worship to God. The splendor and value of heavenly treasures are without measure. Will you dedicate yourself to earthly treasure and forsake heaven? Can there be a more foolish view on life? Heavenly treasure is not only valuable one day, but has significant dividends in this life too.

Lord Jesus, I live in a world that only knows one type of treasure – the one that can be destroyed by moth and vermin and stolen by thieves. I know almost nothing else. Open my eyes to see the heavenly treasures. Amen.

# DISAPPOINTMENT OR SPLENDOR?

*"For where your treasure is, there your heart will be also."*
Matthew 6:21

Where your heart is, there your focus will be. Where your focus is aimed, there your destination will be. Solomon writes: "Above all else, guard your heart, for everything you do flows from it" (Prov. 4:23). What we know as earth is destined to perish. If you put your focus and heart on earthly things, your final destination will also be transient and a great disappointment.

What Jesus is in actual fact saying is, "You might not realize it now, but your final destination is in your hands. Don't be foolish and exchange an eternal and wonderful destination for ash and soot! Turn your heart to God. Focus on the things He focuses on and receive as a reward the splendor of His kingdom without end."

Are you heading for splendor or disappointment? Where do you keep your treasure? Where is your heart? Your focus? Therein lies your final destination. Are you heading for profit or loss? What does God say about your life?

# NO SUCH THING AS "I CAN'T"

*"If you forgive other people when they sin against you, your heavenly Father will also forgive you."*
Matthew 6:14

I've heard people say that this prayer is part of the Old Testament dispensation and not part of God's plans in the New Testament. Then I think, *Show me the person who lives freely from God's grace, forgiveness, reconciliation and righteousness, and still refuses to share these same things and continues to live unharmed and intact in His mercy ...* There is no such thing.

Jesus' parables in Matthew 18 spell it out clearly. If you've received God's forgiveness and life, you have no other choice but to share it, otherwise God will demand accountability. There is no "past tense" about this statement.

Don't ignore or disrespect these words of Jesus. He knows what He's talking about! If you can't forgive others, ask God to forgive you and give you a pure heart. Be obedient without dispute.

# SUCH A HIGH PRICE

*"Look at the birds of the air; they do not sow or reap or store away in barns, and yet your heavenly Father feeds them. Are you not much more valuable than they?"*
Matthew 6:26

The worth of a person is breathtaking! Do you know that nothing, not even sin, can destroy the worth of a person? Achievement (or the lack thereof) doesn't determine your worth. Money, rank, title, culture, origin, race, education, deeds or anything else cannot determine what you're worth.

Only God can determine your value. And do you know how highly God regards people? So much so that He sent His only Son to set us free from sin and death. No creature is valued in this way! *That's* what God thinks of you – with all your faults and shortcomings.

If Satan managed to destroy your self-worth and the value and worth of the people around you, God is not worried. He knows the truth and He will act accordingly.

# FAITH-SPECIFIC MINISTRY

*"Do you believe that I am able to do this?"*
Matthew 9:28

▶ Jesus' ministry was faith specific. His whole ministry and person was aimed at generating faith in people's hearts, but a very specific faith. It wasn't only faith in His abilities, but faith in His person and mission as the Son of God. He was not just a Miracle Worker, but the anointed Son of God.

In effect Jesus asks these blind people: "Do you believe that I am who I say I am?" They answer Him, "Yes, Lord, we believe." Then Jesus replied, "Let what you believe about Me be evident in your lives" and then their blindness was healed! Their testimony was that the Son of God healed them, and not the "sorcerer" of Nazareth.

What do you believe about Jesus? Is it visible through your life? May the Father enable you to see Jesus for who He is! That's the ultimate key.

# DISHONORABLE HONOR

*"I do not accept glory from human beings, but I know you. I know that you do not have the love of God in your hearts."*
John 5:41-42

The Pharisees were furious because Jesus healed someone on the Jewish Sabbath. Accordingly, Jesus answered, "Men, I don't need your approval or recognition. You are busy with your own agenda, not with God's. I know you better than you think. God's love is not in you. All you have is a lifeless religious drive that means nothing to anyone. I won't be guided by you. I'm under God's authority. The same way you treat Him, you will treat Me."

These are heart-stopping words, but true words to those who oppose God. Learn from this. If you're concerned about honor from people, they'll take you down the path they're heading.

Be on your way to God. Be focused on receiving His honor and recognition. If people don't like it, bear with it gladly. Don't deviate from God in order to please people.

# THE DEPTH OF WORSHIP

*He went away a second time and prayed, "My Father, if it is not possible for this cup to be taken away unless I drink it, may Your will be done."*
Matthew 26:42

In the heat of times of crisis and suffering, it's the most natural thing to ask God to spare you from it. But for the child of God there is something more important than being saved from suffering and hardship – the will of God.

The child of God desires to submit to God's will more than they care about being exempt from suffering. "How can suffering ever be the will of God?" you might ask.

Suffering as such is not as important as the consequences of it. Jesus' suffering brought salvation. The disciples' suffering brought about the testimony of the truth of God. God sees the bigger picture. To submit to the will of God is to submit to being a part of this.

Are you willing to submit to God's will even if it means enduring suffering? If yes, your suffering will bring great glory. If not, your suffering will be ineffectual.

# FREE FROM PARASITES

*"Watch and pray so that you will not fall into temptation. The spirit is willing, but the flesh is weak."*
Matthew 26:41

There are two worlds: God's world (the Spirit) and the world of sin (the flesh). The flesh will always rebel against God. It's the nature of sinfulness. The core of temptation is to resist God – to rebel against His authority.

"Be careful," Jesus says, "don't get out of hand. Any remains of the flesh in you will leap at the chance to resist God. Be vigilant and sensitive towards the Holy Spirit in you so that you'll be able to see such opportunities. Any rebellion against God brings about death, but submission to His authority unlocks His glory."

The flesh is not your friend. Don't give any foothold to the devil or the flesh. It's a parasite that will kill you. Stay in God's truth, even if the flesh protests!

# ENDURE INSULTS

*"If anyone slaps you on the right cheek, turn to them the other cheek also."*
Matthew 5:39

Jesus' advice is not to "enjoy pain" or not to defend yourself, but rather to endure insults. To hit someone has more to do with insult than assault. It's situation-specific wisdom. When we are insulted an equally evil and unclean spirit of retribution rises to the fore. We react with as much malice and impurity as the insults we receive. Look at the media for good examples. Disciples of Jesus will rather stand for more insults than to react in an ungodly way. Insult is not to be repaid by insult.

People are responsible for their own actions towards us, but we're also responsible for this before God. Turn the other cheek and allow God to judge accordingly, rather than having to stand guilty before God.

Jesus' disciples live in the truth that Jesus is with them and that He is the Righteous Judge of the nations. Therefore, they can bear unfairness because they know that He will render all justice.

# EXAMINE YOUR HEARTS

*"Yet there are some of you
who do not believe."*
John 6:64

The entire Bible involves *one* thing: believing that Jesus is the Christ and submitting to Him. That is the overall theme, from Genesis to Revelation. In the Old Testament the message was: God will send a Savior. In the New Testament the message is: God *did* send a Savior.

How a person reacts towards this truth determines their whole life and future. Even among the group who followed Jesus, some didn't believe in Him – they just followed. It's the same situation with churches today. The important question is, of course, where do we stand with Jesus? Everything in life is a test of this – do we truly believe in Jesus and do we submit to His authority?

Even though it sounds like we're asking the same question over again, this is what everything is all about. Paul said, "Examine yourselves to see whether you are in the faith; test yourselves" (2 Cor. 13:5).

# A TRUE DISCIPLE

*"You do not want to leave too, do you?" Jesus asked.*
John 6:67

▶ In John 6, Jesus was at His most popular and at the same time the least popular. The one moment the people wanted to make Him king, and the next they all turned their backs on Him.

Many of His disciples left Him and went home. It was then that Jesus posed this question to the group of twelve.

It is the biggest test of faith that every person will have to answer. The first test is: "Follow Me!" The second test is: "Do you want to leave?" There are many things that can disappoint you in your Christian walk – even Christians will offend you. What will you do with Jesus? The follower says, "I've had enough." The disciple says, "Lord, where are we heading? You have the words of spirit and life!"

Many people who have been disappointed by the church also turn their backs on Jesus. I have. But God had mercy on me! How is your test going?

# GOD IN YOUR MIDST

*"The world cannot hate you, but it hates Me because I testify that its works are evil."*

John 7:7

Even Jesus' own brothers didn't believe in Him (see John 7:5). The reason why the world didn't hate them was because they were part of the world, and Jesus wasn't. Jesus' whole being and ministry were light, and darkness hates light.

Hate is a very strong word. It doesn't just mean to dislike. Darkness strongly *hates* the light. Why did Jesus' brothers not believe in Him? The reason was because to them, He was just their older brother, nothing more. His statements that He was the Messiah didn't fit well with them. They were with Jesus, but couldn't recognize who He was. How sad! How tragic!

Lord Jesus, thank You for saving me. May I never find myself in a situation where I'm with You, but don't recognize You. May my heart be vigilant to see You in my midst. Amen.

# FRIEND OR FOE?

*"If you belonged to the world, it would love you as its own. As it is, you do not belong to the world, but I have chosen you out of the world. That is why the world hates you."*
John 15:19

▶ Unlike Jesus' own blood brothers, His disciples looked at Him with different eyes. To them, He was the Son of God, and because of that *they* were not part of the world. This truth is precious. You either oppose Jesus as part of the world, or you stand against the world with Jesus.

For many people their love for the world is just too important, and they choose to stand against Jesus. The big question is: Whose love is worth more? We are all responsible for our own choices. Some people choose the world, saying, "Oh well, God will understand." He will. He understands that you rejected His Son.

The world doesn't remain neutral towards Jesus, but is blatantly hostile. Our choices determine whether we are Jesus' friends or foes. We will have to give account for this before God.

# THE TESTIMONY OF A TRUE DISCIPLE

*"Blessed are those who are per-secuted because of righteousness, for theirs is the kingdom of heaven."*
Matthew 5:10

To do what is right and to love others is the testimony of a true disciple who belongs to God and obeys Him. Persecution is the world's testimony that the disciple belongs to God and obeys Him.

The disciples in Acts were glad that they were deemed worthy to suffer for Jesus. It was, in fact, a great honor, because through this the world acknowledged that they belonged to God, and not to the world. This truth makes one look more vigilantly at the things that happen around you and to you. There is a special blessing on everyone who belongs to Jesus. They are part of God's kingdom, but not the rest.

It can become very lonely when people reject you because you are committed to Jesus. But this loneliness is rewarded with the powerful presence of God. Take heart!

# DON'T LET GO!

*"All this I have told you so that you will not fall away."*
John 16:1

Jesus does not only want us to believe in Him, but also to stay faithful and not turn away from Him. There is a strong possibility of this happening, otherwise He would not have said this. It is true that no one can steal you from God's hand, but it is also true that we can let go of His hand when we don't want to hold on anymore. God doesn't cling to your hand against your will; if you don't want to be with Him, He will let you go.

That's exactly the point: He doesn't want anyone to find themselves in such a situation! The Holy Spirit prepares us to stay faithful to God, no matter what.

Take courage in Jesus' words, "I am coming soon. Hold on to what you have, so that no one will take your crown" (Rev. 3:11).

# GOD KNOWS YOUR HEART

*"Not everyone who says to Me, 'Lord, Lord,' will enter the kingdom of heaven, but only the one who does the will of My Father who is in heaven."*
Matthew 7:21

Jesus clearly distinguishes between religion and discipleship. Religion (more specifically formalism) is more concerned with show than obedience. Churches can be packed with people saying, "Lord, Lord" every Sunday, without any adherence to the authority of God.

Jesus says, "Don't think you can fool God with the right words. God sees through you, and He knows your heart. He only allows those who stand under His authority to enter, not everyone who gives the right answers and who pretends to be religious."

James explains: "Wash your hands, you sinners, and purify your hearts, you double-minded. Grieve, mourn and wail. Change your laughter to mourning and your joy to gloom. Humble yourselves before the Lord, and He will lift you up" (James 4:8-10).

Today's Scripture passage is rather strict, but it's necessary. The message is clear: Stop pretending. Have respect for God and submit to Him.

# STORMS ARE INEVITABLE

*"The rain came down, the streams rose, and the winds blew and beat against that house; yet it did not fall, because it had its foundation on the rock."*
Matthew 7:25

The purpose of faith in Jesus is to obtain access to God's kingdom. It's to remain standing despite the storm, not to exempt you from the storm.

In this life you will experience storms. Jesus speaks of floods and gusts of wind. It's a severe attack on the little house of our lives. But every person has and will experience it. Some houses fall to pieces, while others stand strong and immovable. The difference between collapsing and standing firm is the result of what we do with Jesus' words.

Everything that Jesus says is aimed at making us steadfast. If we obey Him, the storms will not stop, but we will remain standing even in the midst of them.

God takes no pleasure in lives that fall apart. In fact, He wants us to stand firm. Anchor yourself in Jesus, not only today, but every day. It's your only salvation.

# TRUE AND FALSE PURITY

*"Don't you see that nothing that enters a person from the outside can defile them?"*
Mark 7:18

▶ God's definition of being pure is difficult for the world! Religion invented its own complicated system of being pure, with which they try to impress God (actually people). Jesus says, "Don't think that food can make you pure or impure. What you eat goes into your stomach, not your soul, and you get rid of it again.

"However, that which flows from your heart – your thoughts, attitude, words and deeds – shows the condition of your heart. Is it pure or impure before God? Those are the things that determine your purity. Don't condemn people on the basis of what they eat or wear – as if that concludes their purity. You can obey all the demands of formalism and still be impure before God."

How blessed we are to stand pure before God! How blessed we are to be delivered from formalism. How blessed we are to know Jesus – the Cleanser of our hearts and lives. Thank You, Jesus!

# DO GOOD ANYWAY

*"Love your enemies, do good to them, and lend to them without expecting to get anything back. Then your reward will be great, and you will be children of the Most High, because He is kind to the ungrateful and wicked."*
Luke 6:35

▶ Jesus' words are simple: "Do good to the ungrateful and wicked among you, because Your Father also does this." It's nice to do favors for those who are thankful, because they appreciate what we do and can even return the favor. But a life of a disciple is more than this. The Father's children are to imitate Him.

People who are ungrateful and evil don't appreciate our good deeds and will certainly not repay us. Do good deeds anyway. Help where you can. Do good where you can. Your reward is not from people, but from God Himself. If you lend something to someone, do it with the intention to give. Never let anyone "owe" you.

In this way we not only do what God does for us, but we also experience the reality of God who rewards each person according to what he or she has done. Don't disregard God's reward!

# GET TO KNOW GOD

*"God did not send His Son into the world to condemn the world, but to save the world through Him."*
John 3:17

That God will judge the world is a fact, but this is not God's main goal. God lives to save and to reconcile. He wants to bring everyone to salvation so that we can all share in His kingdom. That's what makes His mercy so awesome!

Of course, not everyone wants to be saved and share in God's kingdom. That's the most inconceivable thing. Why would anyone not seize such an opportunity? It's staggering. God says, "I *want* to love you. I *want* to bless you. I *want* to cleanse you and establish you in love. I *don't* want to see you lost. I *don't* want to condemn you. But I *will do* what is right – because that is who I am."

If you think God delights in condemning people, you don't know Him at all! Although His righteous judgment is inevitable, His love is even greater. Get to know Him and His love.

# JUNE

# WORTHY TO BE PRAISED

*"You will look for Me, but you will not find Me; and where I am, you cannot come."*
John 7:34

These words of Jesus have to do with His crucifixion and ministry towards people beyond the grave. It's the one place where only Jesus can go to do what only He can do. His disciples had no insight or entry into this.

There is only one person who is worthy to establish reconciliation for the sins of humanity. That's why He is also called the Lamb of God. It's God's sacrifice to take away the sins of the world. There is another place where Jesus went, and where His disciples can also go. But more about that later. The disciples were overwhelmed by the prospect of the crucifixion, but they didn't understand the miracle that was taking place before their eyes!

Thank You, Lord Jesus, for paying the price for me. Thank You for taking the judgment upon Yourself and saving me from God's wrath, so that I can receive life through Your resurrection. You are worthy to be praised! Amen.

# FIRST BE RECONCILED

*"If you are offering your gift at the altar and there remember that your brother or sister has something against you, leave your gift there in front of the altar. First go and be reconciled to them; then come and offer your gift."*
Matthew 5:23-24

Jesus is serious about this. Purposeful action must be taken when things are done without love. Jesus says, "Listen carefully: there is something more important than your quiet time and to praise and worship. If you've offended (wounded or belittled) anyone with your words or actions, stop what you're doing and be reconciled to them. Otherwise your worship is without effect.

"It will be no use if you wound others and stand before God as if nothing happened. He will not tolerate this. If you do what I ask, your life will be filled with the glory of God. The Father doesn't approve of selfish religious practices. Worship and reconciliation are true worship from a reconciling God."

Take this to heart. Don't allow pride to dictate your actions and attitude. Jesus is Lord – follow Him. The Holy Spirit will assist you in this, but your pride will try to persuade you otherwise.

# THE HEART OF THE FATHER

*"If I go and prepare a place for you, I will come back and take you to be with Me that you also may be where I am. You know the way to the place where I am going."*
John 14:3-4

After Jesus had gone to the place where His disciples couldn't follow Him, He went to where they *could* follow Him – the heart of His Father. That's the place He has prepared for us. That's the purpose of Jesus' whole ministry: to reconcile us with the Father.

Reconciliation doesn't just mean forgiveness. It's more than that. It's forgiveness and an intimate relationship with the God of the universe. And the way there? Through Jesus, of course! He is the way to the heart of the Father. That is the place where Jesus wants to take us with everything He says and does. Jesus rejoices greatly over every person who wants to be reconciled to the Father.

I don't know what kind of relationship you have with your earthly father, but know this: God wants to be your Father! At His bosom is where you belong. You were created for it.

# HOW YOU SHOULD PRAY

*"This, then, is how you should pray:
'Our Father in heaven, hallowed
be Your name.'"*
Matthew 6:9

This sentence overwhelms me. No one could've thought that anyone would be able to address God as Father. This prayer was and still is an absolute revolution in the human understanding of God. The implications of this will fill many publications for years to come.

God's children have one dream: to honor Him in everything they do. They want to see the Father being glorified, not only in their own lives, but through the whole world. That is their reason for living – to be one with God and to see His glory revealed. The first sentence of the Lord's Prayer does not only depict the uniqueness of the disciples' relationship with God, but also their alienation from the world.

To know God as Father and to glorify Him in everything is completely unfamiliar to the world. The gap between the disciples and the secular world is an enormous ravine that can only be bridged by the blood of Jesus.

# ARREST THE INTRUDER

*"'Your kingdom come, Your will
be done, on earth as it is in heaven.'"*
Matthew 6:10

▶ The difference between Jesus' disciples and the world is glaring, isn't it? The world wants to do its own thing, according to its own will, and doesn't accept any authority except its own. Disciples pray for God's authority. They can think of no better world than the one where God is King. They can't think of anything greater than for God's will to be done on earth.

That is Satan and his followers' absolute nightmare! The hope of the church of Jesus Christ is the world's terror. Disciples want no other life than one of submission to God. This unmistakably identifies them as children of the light.

Any tendencies in our lives to resist the will of God are hostile. Take hold of these feelings and lay them before the King. There is no life outside of God's will.

# MORE THAN JUST BIBLE READING AND PRAYER

*"'Give us today our daily bread.'"*
Matthew 6:11

▶ Disciples of Jesus know two things about God. He is their ultimate Provider and they are completely dependent on Him. Being dependent on God doesn't make one weak – on the contrary! There is nothing that gives one more freedom and life than to depend on God.

In this part of the Lord's Prayer, Jesus teaches His disciples to acknowledge this: "We are dependent on You in everything. You are our Source and You are the One who guides us to life." Disciples don't have a "Sunday relationship" with God, but a daily dynamic relationship that entails more than just Bible reading and prayer. They can appreciate God's love and glory in everything. If it goes well, they praise Him; and if not, they remain expectant.

Are you privileged enough to really fathom the fact that your whole being, your breathing, is the result of the miracle of God? Celebrate it!

# DISREGARD FOR GOD'S GRACE

*"'And forgive us our debts, as we also have forgiven our debtors.'"*
Matthew 6:12

"I don't understand. Did God not forgive us according to Jesus' sacrifice on the cross? Why does Jesus then teach His disciples something else?" Yes, God *did* establish our salvation through the blood of Jesus for all our sins. That was the biggest act of mercy ever performed. But that's not all. With it Jesus teaches His disciples that no one can accept God's mercy and goodness, refuse to share it with others, and get away with it.

God undeservingly has mercy on us through Jesus. He expects us to show mercy toward all people, regardless of the circumstances. If we refuse to do this, we're guilty before God for disregarding His mercy and grace.

Don't take forgiveness lightly. To forgive the trespassers in your life is not a suggestion. It's a direct command from the Living God.

# VICTORY FOR SURE!

*"'And lead us not into temptation, but deliver us from the evil one.'"*
Matthew 6:13

Jesus teaches His disciples two very important things: Firstly, God tests, but He can allow us to find ourselves in places where Satan tempts us (like with Jesus in the desert). The prayer above is not that God would not bring us to a place of temptation, but that He would help us to resist it and not fall for the temptation.

Secondly, God always provides a way out (see 1 Cor. 10:13). The prayer further asks that God would deliver us from the evil of Satan's plans. He is a thief, destroyer and slayer. We are not part of Satan's kingdom, but he will try his best to destroy us.

Through this prayer, Jesus' disciples declare that their only victory over Satan is God. We cannot win in own strength, but through God all things are possible.

# THE RIGHTEOUS JUDGE

*"Let any one of you who is without sin be the first to throw a stone at her."*
John 8:7

▶ Jesus says, "Who of you are worthy to judge another? Who of you, who so easily condemn others, also stand guilty before God? If you think you are worthy to be the judge of others, feel free to do so. But know this today: If you condemn this woman and stand guilty too, you will stand under the same judgment.

"The question is not whether what she did was wrong. It was. The question is if you are in any position to execute the sentence! The question is not if sin will be condemned. It will. The question is who will be the one to judge. There is a Judge, but it's not you."

Acknowledge Jesus as the Righteous Judge over all people – and over you. Don't fall into sin and impurity in your search for righteous judgment.

# THE GOLDEN STREET AND THE LIFE-GIVING FOUNTAIN

*"I am the Way and the Truth and the Life. No one comes to the Father except through Me."*
John 14:6

The Church (or body of Christ) is depicted in Revelation as a city on a "mountain great and high" (Rev. 21:10). The Holy City is made of gold, the result of God's work. In this city is a street paved with gold. The author of Hebrews calls it "a new and living way" (Heb. 10:20).

This street leads straight to the throne of God – to the heart of the Father. And when we look at the throne we see a river with living water flowing from the throne and from Christ sitting on the throne. This water is the truth of God who gives life to all who drink it. That's who Jesus is. He is the Golden Street and the Living Water of God's truth. Without Him there is nothing.

The more we learn of Christ, the more we discover how to learn! You can dedicate your whole life to know Jesus without ever exhausting the depth of God.

# OBEY HIM IN ALL THINGS

*"Anyone who loves Me will obey My teaching. My Father will love them, and We will come to them and make Our home with them."*
John 14:23

To take Jesus' words to heart is to obey them. That's how you show that you love Jesus. And then something big happens. The grace and favor of God rests on you and God's presence permeates your life.

This happens on two levels: the one is being born again. When I embrace Jesus as my Savior and Redeemer, God makes His dwelling place in my heart through His Spirit. The second level is His character. The continued obedience of Christ brings God's presence and grace to the furthest corners of my character and everyday life. To embrace Jesus as Lord is not a once-off event. It is a lifestyle characterized by God's power and strength.

Sometimes we pray for things that we can only receive through obedience. Prayer is important, but it's not a substitute for being obedient. Do what Jesus says and experience the power of God in an unprecedented way.

# AT THE ELEVENTH HOUR

*"No one, sir," she said. "Then neither do I condemn you," Jesus declared. "Go now and leave your life of sin."*
John 8:11

I've wondered many times about the things John did not tell us. What went on in the heart of this woman while she awaited her fate before the Pharisees and Jesus? Which things did Jesus know, but not the disciples? Why did Jesus not condemn her sins? Possibly it was because she stood in repentance before Jesus as Lord. At the eleventh hour her heart called out to God and He met her. The Pharisees and even John were completely unaware of this.

In Jesus' justification and redemption of this woman, He revealed one last thing: Forgiveness doesn't mean that your sins are made right. Sin is sin. Stay away from it, leave it and never go back!

Thank You, Father, for forgiving me and cleansing me even at the eleventh hour. Awake within me a deep resentment towards impurity and disobedience, and save me from ever justifying what I do wrong. Amen.

# THE SAME ORIGIN AS CHRIST

*"You are from below; I am from above. You are of this world; I am not of this world."*
John 8:23

▶ It cannot be put any clearer. The words "below" and "above" refer to the origin rather than the geographical location. The origin of words, deeds, thoughts and lifestyle are either from God or from the earth. James qualifies the latter as "earthly, unspiritual, demonic" (James 3:15). There are two systems: the heavenly one under the rule of God and the earthly one under the rule of Satan.

Jesus says, "I'm not of the worldly system. You are. I'm from God's system – you're not. That's why you resist Me." For this reason, being born again is so critical to the gospel of God. Through and in Jesus we die to worldly standards and systems and we are born again into God's system. In this way we have the same origin as Christ.

This is how followers of Christ should encourage each other towards pure lives and eternal hope! We say, "Brother and sister, we are not of this world. We don't live according to worldly standards. We are from Above!"

# POWERFUL PROOF

*"When you have lifted up the Son of Man, then you will know that I am He and that I do nothing on My own but speak just what the Father has taught Me."*
John 8:28

These words are a direct reference to the crucifixion of Jesus and what were to follow. Paul wrote, "Who through the Spirit of holiness was appointed the Son of God in power by His resurrection from the dead: Jesus Christ our Lord" (Rom. 1:4).

The inability of people to recognize Jesus as the Son of God is staggering, but His death and resurrection is indisputable proof that He didn't make an empty claim. He *is* who He said He is, and God confirmed it. The author of Hebrews doesn't say the following for nothing, "How shall we escape if we ignore so great a salvation?" (Heb. 2:3).

The gospel of Jesus is not just another world religion. It is irrevocably established as the only way to God, despite the world trying everything to destroy it.

# OBTAINING THE TRUTH

*"If you hold to My teaching, you are really My disciples. Then you will know the truth, and the truth will set you free."*
John 8:31-32

We receive God's truth in two ways. The initial truth of God comes to us through the gracious ministry of the Holy Spirit. It's true that we are lost without Christ. When we react towards this truth, we are cleansed, saved and restored in our relationship with God.

Hence we can discover the deepest truths of God as we live in obedience to Him. Obedience unlocks the truth in our lives. The more we do His will, the more we discover who He is. And the more we discover Him, the more free we become from the things which bind us. Jesus makes this message very clear. Christianity is not just a "religion," it's an act.

Without God's truth we are bound by the world. For the umpteenth time Jesus invites us, "Do you need life in your marriage, family, business, career, relationships, personal life? Follow Me and do what I say ..."

# TRUE POWER

*"Blessed are the meek, for they will inherit the earth."*
Matthew 5:5

Never confuse gentleness and meekness with having no moral fiber! Gentleness is the ability to stand under God's authority. It's like breaking in a mighty Arab horse to go exactly where the rider wants it to go. If the horse is still wild, it is strong, but cannot be used.

All the promises and blessings from God are available for those who are under His authority. Therein true power and strength can be found. They are God's heirs. Jesus said of Himself, "I am gentle and humble in heart" (Matt. 11:29). If you resist God's authority you can't have a gentle heart and you cannot inherit His blessings.

Be gentle in heart by embracing God's authority. There is no power or blessing in doing only what you want. Allow the Holy Spirit to permeate your soul so you can be useful and powerful.

# TRUE FREEDOM

*"If the Son sets you free,
you will be free indeed."*
John 8:36

Humans strive towards freedom their whole lives. We fight for political freedom, social freedom, economic freedom, freedom of religion … freedom in every single area of human existence.

Still the human race is bound, regardless of all our efforts, successes and endeavors. Jesus explains why. It's only when the Son frees us spiritually that we can experience true freedom. It trumps every other form of human freedom. If Jesus has set you free, you are truly free. This is so even if you're in prison; even if you don't have freedom of speech, social privileges, money or possessions; even if you're being persecuted or killed. Still, you will enjoy the one thing so many have given their lives for: freedom … forever.

Thank You, Lord, for fighting for my freedom – and being victorious! Thank You for truly setting me free to serve God. Thank You for the knowledge that Your freedom for me can never be threatened or destroyed. Amen.

# BLESSED ASSURANCE

*"Very truly I tell you, the one who believes has eternal life."*
John 6:47

Assurance of faith is one of our most pressing questions. How can you know if you're made right before God? How can you know that you're forgiven and not condemned? How can you know that you're going to heaven? I've encountered many people who say that you cannot know. This is just not true.

Jesus differs strongly. His answer is simple: "Whoever surrenders their life over to Me to rule over it; whoever accepts Me as their Shepherd and Master, whoever follows Me is made right in God's eyes. They are forgiven and free from judgment. They have eternal life. If you are with Me you will know for sure!" Jesus brings rest and assurance for our souls. He never leaves us in darkness.

Examine any uncertainty of faith. Maybe you doubt because you're not fully committed to Jesus or because Satan confuses you. Allow Jesus to minister to you. You *can* and *should* know that you are made right before God.

# NO MAGIC FORMULA

*"When you pray, do not keep on babbling like pagans, for they think they will be heard because of their many words."*

Matthew 6:7

Prayer is not a magic formula, though many people think it is. You can hear it when they pray. Some think that fancy words, the repetition of "Jesus" or "Amen" or "Hallelujah," or deep, long prayers will be more favorably accepted by God.

Other people think that the correct order of words or the exact repetition of the Lord's Prayer (or any other prayer) will achieve the desired effect. Jesus dismisses all these things as untrue. His advice to His disciples is: "Talk to your Father – don't try magic tricks. Talk to God. Don't try to sell Him something. Speak from your heart and without pretense. Nobody likes pretense – including God."

Listen to your prayers next time you pray. Do you talk normally? Are you sincere? Do you talk to your Father as some far-off, impersonal god? Do you talk like a child or a stranger to your Father?

# END OF STORY

*"If God were your Father, you would love Me, for I have come here from God. I have not come on My own; God sent Me."*
John 8:42

Jesus put it to the Jews that the only proof that God is your Father is if you've accepted Jesus as Savior and love Him. Then He said, "Here I am. What will it be? You're quick to speak, but prove your claims. You say you serve God and love Him – prove it by accepting Me. Let's not fight. Let's settle the matter here and now."

How many times do people say, "It's not just you who serve God? I also pray and read the Bible. I might not be the leader of the pack in church, but you don't know what goes on inside my heart!" Good. Prove it. Are you under God's authority – yes or no? End of story.

You don't *have* to stand under Jesus' authority. He gives you a choice, but you can't claim a relationship with God while rejecting Jesus' authority.

# A PURE AND GENTLE HEART

*"Why is My language not clear to you? Because you are unable to hear what I say."*
John 8:43

Why not? What prevents them? Who was Jesus addressing? It was the religious Jews of Jesus' time. Although religious, they had no delight in serving God. Accordingly, they could not acknowledge Jesus for who He was.

The leaders denied Him, and resisted everything He said. By so doing, their eyes and mind stayed shut to God's message. They heard Jesus' words, but had no insight into what He was talking about. There was nothing wrong with their intellect – it was their hearts that were unreceptive. They were literally willfully deaf and only saw what they wanted to see. They could therefore not understand what Jesus was saying.

What goes on in our hearts determines our whole lives. This includes being able to receive from God, and to understand what He says. Guard your heart. Keep it pure and gentle before God.

# REST A WHILE

*"Come with Me by yourselves to a quiet place and get some rest."*
Mark 6:31

► Isn't it significant that Jesus took His disciples to a quiet place to rest for a bit? It's possible to work very hard and yet achieve nothing. God didn't only create us to work and be busy. He also made us to rest.

There is no reward in working for years on end without resting. Some people boast about it. But it's not *more* spiritual. Even Jesus, with only three years of ministering on earth, rested and taught His disciples to do the same thing. Are we better than our Master? No. Learn from Jesus how to become quiet and rest. It doesn't make you less productive. "The blessing of the Lord brings wealth, without painful toil for it" (Prov. 10:22).

People who realize their dependence on God are people who can also submit to rest.

# JESUS IS THE NEW TESTAMENT

*"Do not think that I have come to
abolish the Law or the Prophets;
I have not come to abolish
them but to fulfill them."*
Matthew 5:17

One of the greatest revelations of Jesus' ministry is that He is the absolute fulfillment of the Old Testament. The New Testament replaced the Old Testament, not by closing it, but by fulfilling it.

Jesus is the New Testament. He is the Perfect Finisher of everything God said. In Him God's promises are "Yes" and "Amen" (see 2 Cor. 1:20). There is nothing in the Old Testament that Jesus didn't fulfill. Therefore, the New Testament believers are not "bound" by the Old Testament, but rather associated with Christ who is the fulfillment thereof. Christ is the new law of God. This is a truth that takes a lifetime to be appreciated!

People sometimes try to do what Jesus has already done, namely to fulfill the terms and conditions of the Old Testament. Take hold of Jesus and you take hold of everything that God has ever said!

# IDENTIFICATION

*"Whoever belongs to God hears what God says. The reason you do not hear is that you do not belong to God."*
John 8:47

How does one distinguish between true children of God and those who claim to be, but aren't? Jesus makes it clear: Children of God do what He says because the Spirit dwells in them.

Previously, when they were children of the world, they resisted God in everything. But matters changed drastically. Something happened – supernatural change took place. Now they *want* to be obedient.

That is how you can identify the true and the false. The one group doesn't tolerate any excuses for being disobedient to God; the other group thinks of excuses all the time for why they aren't. The one group's honor lies in obedience; the other's in evasion.

The kingdom of God is not one of speeches and rhetoric. It's a Kingdom of action! Children of God wear identification documents of obedience. They're incontestable.

# BEFORE ABRAHAM

*"Very truly I tell you,"*
*Jesus answered, "before*
*Abraham was born, I am!"*
John 8:58

Of all the things that Jesus said, this statement was perhaps one of the most glaring to the religious, unbelieving Jews. It is a statement unequivocally proclaiming Jesus' deity.

Jesus says, "You make such a fuss about Abraham, but what you don't know is that I called Abraham. I appeared to him. I told him that he was going to have a son. I asked him why he laughed at Sarah and I gave him an offering to take the place of his son, Isaac. I existed long before Abraham and am far above him."

The revelation of who Jesus Christ really is, is far greater than what the world knows. They might dismiss Him as just another religious leader of His time, but we see Him as God, without beginning or end.

# GREAT GLORY

*"Very truly I tell you, unless a kernel of wheat falls to the ground and dies, it remains only a single seed. But if it dies, it produces many seeds."*
John 12:24

▶ There is a principle in God's kingdom that is important to understand: Life comes through death. Traditionally we see death as the end, but God looks at it differently. Nothing good comes from the workings of the flesh; it's the Spirit of God who brings glory and blessings.

The zeal of man yields no godly harvest. This zeal and workings must die, so that God can bring life through His Spirit. A kernel of wheat has to die before it can produce many seeds. We will experience this principle many more times in our lives. Often our own plans and efforts must die so that God's plans can be realized. It might be painful to us, but the end result is great glory!

Pray less earnestly for your own plans and thoughts to stay alive. Rather pray for the speedy death of the kernel of wheat so that God's glory can produce a wonderful crop.

# GO INTO
# ALL THE WORLD

*"Therefore go and make disciples of all nations, baptizing them in the name of the Father and of the Son and of the Holy Spirit, and teaching them to obey everything I have commanded you. And surely I am with you always, to the very end of the age."*

Matthew 28:19-20

Here the disciples received their godly mandate to spread the gospel. Jesus' command is very specific. The focus of the command is not only to preach and to convert people. It is specifically focused on making followers and disciples of Jesus – people who do what He says.

This is far removed from religiosity and "good church-goers." Jesus speaks about fellowship of people completely focused on obeying Him in the finest details of their lives. That is what the disciples were to focus on. They weren't only expected to establish churches and do missionary work, they had to exemplify Jesus to everyone they met.

Don't follow spiritual trends of the times. Don't advocate your own denomination. Follow Jesus. Be an ardent campaigner for absolute obedience to Him.

# AUTHORITY AND POWER

*"I want you to know that the Son of Man has authority on earth to forgive sins."*
Mark 2:10

▶ There is only One who can forgive sins, because there is only One Lamb of God. There is only One Mediator between God and people, because there is only One worthy to do this. That Person is Jesus Christ. It's not the reverend or the pastor or those who are "holy." It's not religion or the church. It's also not a movement or an organization.

Jesus doesn't share His authority with anyone. He has the authority and power. To reject Jesus is to reject God's forgiveness. To reject God's forgiveness is to assure your own condemnation.

To follow Jesus is to embrace everything that God wants to give us – forgiveness, blessings, protection, reconciliation, restoration and salvation. Outside of Jesus we have no access to these things.

# WORSE THAN BEING BLIND

*"For judgment I have come into this world, so that the blind will see and those who see will become blind."*
John 9:39

▶ It's easy to grasp that Jesus came to earth to enlighten spiritually blind people, but how did His coming also bring blindness to those who *can* see? Jesus spoke to those who claimed to have spiritual insight. They bragged about the fact that they understood God and were close to Him, but their fame was not founded in Jesus. Their insight was in truth no insight at all and their claims were empty.

They proclaimed a "gospel" based on their own culture and preferences. They showed zeal for God, but practiced a "God-less" religion. People like this will never find insight into God unless they realize that they're blind. They must first become "blind" before they can "see".

Someone who is blind can't see, but someone who is blind and convinced that they can in fact see is completely lost. Pray that Jesus will keep your heart from this!

# NO GREATER PRIVILEGE

*"The sheep listen to his voice. He calls his own sheep by name and leads them out."*
John 10:3

▶ Isn't it wonderful that the Shepherd knows your name? Jesus is not just speaking to the crowd. He is speaking personally and intimately. You might not be someone important to the people around you, but to Jesus you're important enough to know personally.

He calls your name. Do you hear it? Listen. There it is again! The reason why He's calling you is to lead you to quiet waters and green pastures. He wants to care for you and minister to you. Don't pull away. You only rob yourself of the things you long for most. Listen to Jesus and follow Him. He is not just *the* Shepherd, He's *your* Shepherd.

Jesus' flock is not an organization, but a relationship. Jesus doesn't organize believers. He has a relationship with each one and walks with them personally. There's no greater privilege than this!

JULY

# THE SHEPHERD'S VOICE

*"They will never follow a stranger; in fact, they will run away from him because they do not recognize a stranger's voice."*

John 10:5

True disciples' eyes are wide open, because Jesus opened them. In the past they couldn't distinguish between all the voices they heard and followed anyone and anything, but not anymore!

They now not only know how to run to the Shepherd, but also how to run from those who pretend to be the Shepherd. Sweet words, empty promises and placatory voices no longer attract them.

Only the voice of their Shepherd draws them in, a voice they know well. Wherever they hear His voice, there they are safe. If they don't hear Him, then they run.

Don't lend your ears to those claiming to be the Shepherd. They want to trap you with their open-mindedness. Disciples of Jesus are not open-minded; they're single-minded.

# A SPIRITUAL BLACK MARKET

*"I am the gate; whoever enters through Me will be saved. They will come in and go out, and find pasture."*
John 10:9

There is only one way to receive the things from God that you long for, and that is through His Son, Jesus. He is the door to everything God has planned for you and me. There is no such thing as a spiritual black market where you can buy things for cheap or get hold of it quicker or easier.

The spiritual black market will only trade your soul for garbage. Jesus, on the other hand, will save your soul and treasure it. People who desperately want to be successful are often seen browsing the black market for a "blessing" or two. But people who are truly successful have surrendered everything over to Jesus and steadfastly hold on to Him – even if it means losing everything. They are immovable, even in crises – not because they're great, but because the Shepherd looks after them.

Stay with Jesus. There is no other option. Go through the only entrance to God's heart – Jesus – and stay there!

# LIFE IN ABUNDANCE

*"The thief comes only to steal and kill and destroy; I have come that they may have life, and have it to the full."*
John 10:10

The contrast between the works of Satan and Jesus' ministry is stark. Satan utilizes unlimited violence and evil to rob people of their lives, in the same way that sheep are slaughtered and the last bit of life and joy sucked from them.

Conversely, Jesus gave His life so that we can live through Him. He doesn't take life, He gives it. He doesn't kill and destroy, He saves and blesses.

Satan doesn't treat anyone well, except to lure them in to destroy them. Jesus gives life in abundance. He gives more than we can use!

Stay away from places where Satan roams free. He will not leave you unscathed. Teach your children to do likewise.

# ON GOD'S SIDE

*"I have other sheep that are not of this sheep pen. I must bring them also. They too will listen to My voice, and there shall be one flock and one shepherd."*
John 10:16

I've heard people say that Jesus was talking about other religions in today's Scripture verse, and that all roads lead to God. That's not true. Other religions are not addressed here. Jesus is speaking to the Jews and He says that His disciples are not only Jews, but are from other nations, cultures and languages.

The Church of Jesus Christ consists of all nations and He wants to unite His flock as one. Jesus is not culturally limited. He is not only Jewish, Afrikaans, American, Zulu or Chinese. He is Lord over all the earth and everyone who is committed to Him is united in Him. There is one Lord over all; any other opinions don't come from God and must be rejected.

People often claim God for themselves. God must be on *our* side. He isn't. He's on His own side. We are either with Him or against Him.

# DEATH, WHERE IS YOUR STING?

*"This sickness will not end in death.
No, it is for God's glory so that
God's Son may be glorified
through it."*
John 11:4

Isn't it interesting that Lazarus, of whom Jesus is talking here, did in fact die? Did Jesus not say that his sickness would not end in death? When the disciples asked Jesus about it, He said, "Lazarus had fallen asleep" (v. 11). You know the rest of the story.

Was God's glory revealed? Was the Son glorified through it? Did Lazarus rise from the grave? Without a doubt. Not only are the words of Jesus true, but they also show that death holds no threat over Him.

To Jesus, death is no formidable enemy. People fear death, but to Him death is a defeated foe.

There is no one like Jesus! There is no threat when you're with Jesus. Hold this truth in your heart and mind. You don't have to try and be brave. Just stand by the King.

# LORD OVER DEATH AND LIFE

*"Lazarus is dead, and for your sake I am glad I was not there, so that you may believe. But let us go to him."*
John 11:14-15

When Jesus comforted the disciples by saying that Lazarus had only fallen asleep, they didn't quite understand what He was saying. Then He said plainly, "Friends, Lazarus is not sleeping in the way you think. He is dead. I'm glad about it, because today I'm going to show you who I really am.

"It's important for you to see this, because you need to believe in Me. I have the power to heal the sick and forgive sins, but I can also wake the dead, because I'm Lord over death and life. Come with Me and I'll show you ..." How fortunate were the disciples? The revelation of who Jesus really is was the most important event in their lives.

This is still the most important event of our lives. Without it we have no faith, hope or life. Pray now for Jesus to reveal Himself to you in power so that you will truly see Him.

# NO GREATER COMFORT

*"I am the resurrection and the life. The one who believes in Me will live, even though they die; and whoever lives by believing in Me will never die. Do you believe this?"*
John 11:25-26

Throughout the ages, life on earth hasn't changed that much. We might live more comfortably than a century ago, but evil is still rampant. Death is everywhere. That's why our homes look like prisons. We protect our lives at all costs, but even then we don't always succeed. We fight a constant battle against evil.

One thing is for sure: we *will* die – even if it's of old age. What Jesus is in fact saying is that in Him we will live, even though we die. In Him the biggest threat on earth is not life-threatening anymore. In Him nothing can steal the life that God gives – even though we die. There is no greater safety and security than this.

To the world the message is this: "Do what you please, but it won't destroy us. In Jesus we are safe, even though we die. Nothing has power over us, not even death."

# TROUBLED, BUT NOT FEARFUL

*"Now My soul is troubled, and what shall I say? 'Father, save Me from this hour'? No, it was for this very reason I came to this hour. Father, glorify Your name!"*
John 12:27-28

▶ God's truth is unmasked. Jesus doesn't pretend to be unaffected by arrest, torture or death. He doesn't have to. His spirituality is not based on pretense, but on His knowledge and faith in the Father. His grisly prospect was part of His calling, yet His only concern was that God would be glorified in everything. He had faith that God would carry Him through it all.

There is a difference between being troubled and being fearful. Jesus was upset, but not filled with fear. He didn't fear, because He believed in the Father. He was troubled, because that's what rejection does to a person. Still His focus was fixed: to do the will of the Father, no matter what.

Don't fret about your troubled heart. Acknowledge it and allow God to minster to you. Stand firm on this one thing: no matter how troubled your soul, hold fast to what God said so that He can be glorified by it.

# OUR ONLY HOPE

*"Anyone who loves their life will lose it, while anyone who hates their life in this world will keep it for eternal life."*
John 12:25

To choose Jesus can often bring one into conflict with what one really wants and what the world offers. The question is always: Whom will you choose? Will you choose Jesus, no matter what; or will you exchange Jesus for your own safety, desires and worldly promises?

Jesus makes it simple: "If you give Me up for anything else, you will lose your life. I'm your only hope of life. If you give Me up in exchange for your own life, you will lose it.

"I'm not exchangeable, because I am Life. Rather choose to be killed instead of forsaking Me. In this way, you're guaranteed life. Nothing can replace Me."

At this very moment, millions of disciples of Jesus are being persecuted. In other places disciples are lured by success if they would only forsake Him. How will you respond?

# THE RIGHT CHOICES

*"Repent therefore! Otherwise, I will soon come to you and will fight against them with the sword of My mouth."*
Revelation 2:16

The sword of Jesus' mouth is the words that He speaks. These words can prune you to bear more fruit, but it can also bring God's judgment over a situation. While Jesus was saying these words, He was pruning the church. They had to learn what to do with the false teachings in their midst. But to the people spreading these false teachings, His words did nothing.

They are also a warning of eminent wrath and condemnation. Jesus is the Judge over all the nations and the Head and Protector of the Church. Nobody will touch His church without Him acting on it. His words are not empty threats; He has the authority to act and He will do exactly that.

Jesus' words bring life to those who embrace them, but to those who reject them, they bring death. The choice is yours, as well as the consequences.

# NO BETTER NAME

*"Unless I wash you, you have no part with Me."*
John 13:8

If you haven't been cleansed by Jesus, you have no part in God's salvation. There is no god, religion or other way or means to be restored and forgiven in order to stand pure before God.

To belong to Jesus is to share in all the blessings and salvation that God has in store for us. That is the world's biggest problem with Jesus: "How can He claim to be the only righteous One – that only He can cleanse us? Who is He to say such things?"

He is the Son of God. He is on equal footing with the Father. He is the only plan of salvation.

How can everyone go to hell who doesn't believe like you do? It's not you who would send anyone there. If anyone needs to be sent, Jesus will do it. Just believe what Jesus says, because we know who He is.

# NOW YOU KNOW!

*"Now that you know these things, you will be blessed if you do them."*
John 13:17

Jesus says, "You know now who I am. You know what I want. You know My commands. You've seen My example. The road has been demonstrated and spelled out to you. It's not enough to only know these things. Now you must walk this road. God's blessing rests on walking this way.

"If you walk this way, God's presence will surround you. If you don't, you're worse off than the world who doesn't know these things.

"The world will be condemned because they rejected Me, but if you know the way but don't walk in it, you'll be held doubly responsible. Don't let anything hold you back from following Me."

If something holds you back, whatever it is, lay it before Jesus' feet and pray for deliverance. He is faithful to grant you life in every way. You know this now – and you'll be blessed if you do it!

# JESUS' LEGACY

*"My Father's house has many rooms;
if that were not so, would I have
told you that I am going there
to prepare a place for you?"*
John 14:2

Years ago, I thought Jesus was talking about a place in heaven where He'll be taking me one day. If you read the passage carefully, you'll see that's not exactly right.

Jesus says, "Don't worry about the fact that I will be crucified. Through it I am going to open up the way for you to come close to the Father's heart. I'm going to make it possible for you to be part of God's family.

"When the Father resurrects Me, I'm going to take you to be with Him – you're going to be part of Our family. That is God's plan for you. If this wasn't true, I wouldn't have said it."

The best place in the universe to be is at the heart of the Father. There is no greater privilege than to be part of God's family. That's Jesus' legacy for you and me!

# STUBBORN OR PROUD?

*"Settle matters quickly with your adversary who is taking you to court. Do it while you are still together on the way, or your adversary may hand you over to the judge, and the judge may hand you over to the officer, and you may be thrown into prison. Truly I tell you, you will not get out until you have paid the last penny."*
Matthew 5:25-26

▶ Have you ever been wrong because of something you've said or done, but you were very reluctant to admit it and even defended it? (Of course the answer for all people is "yes!")

Jesus says, "An attitude like this is going to cost you dearly. It doesn't just promise to burden you with worries, but will also completely destroy your integrity. Listen to God's advice: what is wrong is wrong. If you're wrong, admit it. It's the road to healing and deliverance. It doesn't matter what others have done wrong. You stand before God with your own life, just like them. Admit your wrongs and make things right without being stubborn."

No argument is as powerful as this: "I was wrong, I admit it." Who can stand against that? Pride will destroy you, while humility will keep you in good standing forever, God says.

# FIND JOY IN THE LORD

*"I will not leave you as orphans; I will come to you. Before long, the world will not see Me anymore, but you will see Me. Because I live, you also will live."*
John 14:18-19

▶ "Before long" refers to Jesus' resurrection and close relationship with believers, of whom the world will have no part. The disciples were worried that they would be left all alone when Jesus died.

Jesus says, "Not at all! The great adventure only starts *after* My resurrection! I'm going to leave you for a little while, but after My resurrection no one will ever be able to separate Me from you ever again. I will be with you for all eternity! The world will not see Me anymore, but you will see and experience Me every day like never before. Like Me, you'll also live for eternity and no one will be able to destroy your eternal life!"

Don't allow the world's blindness to become your blindness. Jesus really is with you. May the Holy Spirit open your eyes to see Jesus and find joy therein.

# NEW WINE AND NEW WINESKINS

*"They pour new wine into new wineskins."*
Mark 2:22

The "new wine" is the new ministry of Jesus in the New Testament. The "new wineskins" are the new dispensation of the New Testament. The "old wine" is the ministry of God before the coming of Jesus – the precursor of what was to follow. With the birth of Jesus, the Father introduced "new wine" into "new wineskins."

People did not know this, however. Although they welcomed the newness of Jesus' ministry, they tried to fit this into the Old Testament system and that didn't work. "Old wineskins" burst and break all the time.

Jesus is very clear: "Pour the new wine into new wineskins!" The first wine and wineskins played a significant role, but God introduced a new era.

Father, we thank You for the "new wine" of Jesus' ministry. Open our eyes to see and understand the "new wineskins." Amen.

# A DEAD SYSTEM

*"The Sabbath was made for man,*
*not man for the Sabbath."*
Mark 2:27

▶ The word *religion* in Latin means "respect for what is sacred," but people's understanding of it and what we've done with it diminished the meaning of the word. Now it rather means: "That which people have decided must be respected."

Religion is a dead, human burden that enslaves people. It gives no life, only the "security" of enslavement.

People often use the things of God to add to their own belief systems, giving them greater authority. In this way people *think* they're serving God, but they're actually serving themselves. On various occasions Jesus pointed this out. "Come to Me first" was His counter offer.

Does religion also wear you out? You're not the only one! Jesus is not a religion – He is the Living Way to God. Allow Him to show you the way and teach you the things of God.

# SENSELESS WORRYING

*"Can any one of you by worrying add a single hour to your life?"*
Matthew 6:27

▶ Worry is like a wood beetle: it eats at you from the inside out and happens spontaneously. Jesus asks a good question: "What does it help to worry? It brings no solutions. It doesn't change matters. It just makes you sick. Worry aggravates your emotions and thoughts. And for what?

"By worrying you become driven by fear. If you grasp the truth that God watches over you and that your life is in His hands, you'll stop worrying. Your Father knows what you need. Do you know that unbelief is the best incubator for worry? Don't fall for Satan's 'what ifs.' Trust the Father. There *will* be troubles, but God is bigger than them."

If worrying has become a habit, you're in trouble! Rather get in the habit of trusting God. He is faithful. Practice this in every crisis and difficult situation, and exchange worry for trust.

# THE LAST WORD

*"Stand up in front of everyone."*
Mark 3:3

To the man with the shriveled hand this was the answer to his prayers. For the Pharisees it was just a trap. Would Jesus fulfill the will of the Father even if it is used against Him? Jesus' words leave no doubt!

Self-protection is often our greatest enemy, because it leads us to disobey God. Jesus did what the Father asked. The man with the shriveled hand was healed and the Pharisees received the ammunition they were looking for.

Obedience to God means to be willing to bear the consequences. There will always be consequences. Darkness will always react – but so will God.

Don't consider people's reactions when you obey God. Be fearless in your obedience, regardless of the consequences. God always has the last word.

# DON'T LIVE BACKWARDS

*"But seek first His kingdom and His righteousness, and all these things will be given to you as well."*
Matthew 6:33

▶ Priorities, priorities! If you come across an accident scene, what is the first thing to do? Do you try to stop the bleeding of the victim, or first comb his hair? That's exactly Jesus' point. We are often so intensely involved in the less important things that we pour all our energy and time into them.

Jesus says, "Friends, it's a matter of prioritizing. Strive to be under God's authority and do what He says. It will set everything in your lives straight. Don't live backwards. Don't do your own thing and then ask for God's blessing. First ask God what He wants you to do, then you will receive the blessing you need."

The authority of God in your daily life is what it's all about. It doesn't matter what your profession is or who you are or where you come from. Dedicate yourself to doing God's will and see what He can do through you!

# THE WRITING ON THE WALL

*"If a house is divided against itself, that house cannot stand."*
Mark 3:25

▶ Although Jesus' words were meant to explain why He didn't drive out the devil, it's a very valid and general truth. We spend lots of money and incalculable amounts of energy protecting our families, yet we can be the biggest reason why our families are destroyed.

Selfishness and pride in our hearts can bring about so much division and separation behind the alarm systems and burglar bars that we bring about our own demise in the end.

Unity within a family is not achieved when everyone does what he or she wants, but rather when everyone is subject to God's authority. If parents don't model this to their children, the writing is on the wall.

It's not only a parent's greatest task to see that their children obey God, but to also model a life dedicated to God.

# NO HONOR IN BEING UNWISE

*"Do not give dogs what is sacred; do not throw your pearls to pigs. If you do, they may trample them under their feet, and turn and tear you to pieces."*
Matthew 7:6

In this Scripture passage, Jesus taught His disciples to show discernment when they dealt with the gospel. It can be very unwise to share the gospel with someone who actively resists it. They may make a mockery of what is precious to God and what belongs to Him. You cannot pray for a closed flower to open up – this is the work of the Holy Spirit.

Show discernment in specific situations and refrain from dealing with God's treasure in an unwise manner. Rather focus on people who are receptive. Reveal God's truths with them so that they can also share in all that God has to offer. Be careful not to dishonor God and bring unnecessary mockery on Him.

Read Jesus' advice in Luke 10:4-12. Apply these truths in your discussions on social and public media!

# SEEK, KNOCK, ASK!

*"Which of you, if your son asks
for bread, will give him a stone?
Or if he asks for a fish, will give him
a snake? If you, then, though you are
evil, know how to give good gifts to your
children, how much more will your Father in
heaven give good gifts to those who ask Him!"*
Matthew 7:9-11

After Jesus' warning in verse 6, the assurance comes in verses 7-11. Will God give you the wisdom you need to get by? Will you give your son a stone if he asks for bread? Certainly not. How much more will your Father in heaven give good gifts, like wisdom, if you ask Him! Just ask. He will never leave you to your own devices.

He grants us mercy and grace to live and thrive. That's the heart of the Father. Seek, knock, ask! He is ready to minister to you. Have faith in His love. If even bad people give good things to their children, surely the Father will exceed those good gifts by a very long way!

James repeated this advice to believers in later years in James 1:5: "If any of you lacks wisdom, you should ask God, who gives generously to all without finding fault, and it will be given to you."

# BLASPHEMY AGAINST THE SPIRIT

*"Whoever blasphemes against the Holy Spirit will never be forgiven; they are guilty of an eternal sin."*
Mark 3:29

The main purpose of the Holy Spirit is to reveal Jesus as the Son of God and the Savior of the world to people. To blaspheme against the Spirit is to reject this revelation and any chance of salvation and forgiveness.

All sins, no matter how inconceivable, can be forgiven. The blood of Jesus paid for it. But there is no forgiveness or way out when God is rejected.

Even the people's rejection of Jesus of Nazareth will be forgiven, but the rejection of the revelation of who Jesus really is, is without forgiveness. As long as people reject this truth, they will find no salvation, but when they embrace this revelation they will be completely restored by God!

Blasphemy against the Holy Spirit is exactly this. No one who embraces the revelation of Jesus can blaspheme against the Spirit. Those who reject this revelation are guilty.

# "I PRAY AND READ MY BIBLE TOO"

*"These people honor Me with their lips, but their hearts are far from Me."*

Mark 7:6

▶ In this Scripture passage, Jesus is quoting from the book of Isaiah. It's the core of human religion – exactly the opposite of what Jesus wants.

Religion gives a lot of lip service. We say the right things and do the right things at face value. We go to church, but do what we want. We are chosen to serve on the church council, but we're not chosen by God. We pay attention to everything besides what God wants.

He wants the obedience and love of our hearts. People are quick to say, "I pray and read my Bible too," without any intention to obey God. He sees and knows all things and is appalled by this.

True worship comes from a life dedicated to God by obedience. It's the only form of worship that is pleasing to God. Anything else is false.

# "WHAT WOULD JESUS DO?"

*"They worship Me in vain; their teachings are merely human rules. You have let go of the commands of God and are holding on to human traditions."*
Mark 7:7-8

Jesus continues with His quotation from the book of Isaiah. It's often difficult to distinguish between the teachings of God and mere human rules.

Everyone claims to understand and apply the Bible in the right way. God's command is to love – something that we as humans don't (or cannot) pay much attention to. Jesus says that human traditions are worthless. They don't bring the human heart any closer to God. They only soothe our own ignorance. People are much more concerned about keeping their own teachings and traditions than following God. Jesus' disciples, however, need to take a different approach.

Disciples never say, "But we've always done it this way." They rather say, "What would Jesus do? What did He teach us? Is what is happening here true to the Person and character of Jesus?"

# TALK IS CHEAP

*"By their fruit you will recognize them."*
Matthew 7:20

►We've touched on this Scripture passage, but I want to elaborate on it. Many people want to speak on God's behalf. Others say, "Thus says the Lord." Some speak from the pulpit, others speak their minds on Internet forums, and some write books.

Some people attend Bible study and prayer meetings. Others send emails and text messages. And some people witness on behalf of God. How can we distinguish between true prophets of God and self-appointed false prophets?

Jesus says that the test lies in the fruit they bear: their actions. If they live according to Jesus' will, they belong to God, but if they uphold some other lifestyle they are not from God. Don't be fooled by words. Seek integrity in a person's way of life. Jesus' life and His attitude are the model to follow.

It might be difficult to know how some people really live their lives, but trust God for wisdom. A person can't hide their true colors forever.

# CONCERNED ABOUT APPEARANCE

*"Many will say to Me on that day,
'Lord, Lord, did we not prophesy
in Your name and in Your name drive
out demons and in Your name perform
many miracles?' Then I will tell them plainly,
'I never knew you. Away from Me, you evildoers!'"*
Matthew 7:22-23

Jesus confirms His teaching about integrity and daily living. The fact that someone preaches, casts out demons and performs miracles is not indisputable proof that the person belongs to Jesus. One can easily be misled.

Jesus' words "I never knew you" and "Get away from Me" send shivers down one's spine. Through people's rebellion, they distance themselves from Jesus. Now Jesus distances Himself from them. Even worse is the fact that Jesus says, "Many will say to Me on that day …"

Jesus is aware of the fact that many people stand under the banner of His ministry, but rebel against Him. It emphasizes Jesus' earlier advice: "Don't live your life backwards!" (see Matt. 6:33).

God doesn't tolerate false appearances. He is concerned about a sincere life of obedience that is dedicated to Him. Don't be so worried about appearances, rather focus on complete obedience to God through Jesus.

# BUILD CORRECTLY!

*"Everyone who hears these words of Mine and does not put them into practice is like a foolish man who built his house on sand. The rain came down, the streams rose, and the winds blew and beat against that house, and it fell with a great crash."*
Matthew 7:26-27

Precious, wonderful words! Jesus says, "Friends, life is full of drama! There will always be storms. No life is exempt from them. I'm not here to save you from all the storms of life, but to help you stand firm in the midst of them.

"Listen to My advice. Don't just hear My words. Do what I say. This will establish a firm foundation and build character so you will be able to withstand any storm. But if you just hear and My advice doesn't show through your actions, you'll develop a false sense of security. When the storms of life hit you, you'll fall flat to the ground. Only wounds and destruction will remain."

Don't pray for the storms of life to disappear. Rather choose to be faithful and obedient. That is Jesus' advice to you. His power is revealed in the midst of the storm!

# SACRED COWS

*"You have a fine way of setting aside the commands of God in order to observe your own traditions!"*
Mark 7:9

▶ When your heart is set on doing something your own way, it will devise plans to distort God's words to suit you best.

In this way people often take God's words and use them for their own denomination, race, politically orientated plans, and their own desires.

People shape God's arguments in astonishing ways – in order to do their own thing in their own way. Why do we do that? It's surely not to fool God, because He can't be fooled. Do we do it to fool ourselves and to soothe our own conscience? And possibly to find "reasons" not to obey God?

Father, are there "sacred cows" in my life – things that I artistically use to shift Your commands aside? I don't want to sustain anything that is not from You. Amen.

# LOSING IN ORDER TO WIN?

*"Whoever finds their life will lose it,
and whoever loses their life for
My sake will find it."*
Matthew 10:39

How we live our lives can lead to tension and stress, but if we understand God's ways, we will receive His peace – peace even in the midst of great crises.

The principle is simple: In our efforts for survival and success, we take control of our own lives at the expense of God's will and truth. Such endeavors lead to destruction. However, if we submit our survival and success to God's will and truth, it will lead to our preservation.

In other words, don't follow your natural instinct! It always leads away from God and towards destruction. Shamelessly take hold of Jesus. Don't allow yourself to come undone. Cling to Him and to life. If you lose Him, you lose everything.

Lord Jesus, may my eyes be opened like Peter when I'm cornered to either confirm or deny You. May I never put my own selfish interests before Your reputation! Amen.

# AUGUST

# CLEVER ENOUGH TO VETO GOD

*"I praise You, Father, Lord of heaven and earth, because You have hidden these things from the wise and learned, and revealed them to little children. Yes, Father, for this is what You were pleased to do."*
Matthew 11:25-26

Why would God do this? Does He not want everyone to come to repentance and be saved? (see 1 Tim. 2:4). The answer doesn't lie in God's attitude or character, but in ours.

It's not wrong to be clever and educated, but the pride that often goes with it is wrong. The moment people receive knowledge and information, they think they know enough to veto God. James wrote, "God opposes the proud but shows favor to the humble" (James 4:6).

God doesn't love informed people more than the uninformed. He just withholds Himself from the proud who think they know more while they reject the God of all wisdom and knowledge. God reveals Himself to the humble and dependent because that is His gracious intention.

Pride doesn't mean differing with God. Remove pride from your heart and experience Him!

# BE WARNED

*"If any of you has a sheep and it falls into a pit on the Sabbath, will you not take hold of it and lift it out? How much more valuable is a person than a sheep! Therefore it is lawful to do good on the Sabbath."*
Matthew 12:11-12

When the Bible talks about the flesh, it talks about everything in human nature that is not from the Spirit of God. The flesh is earthly, natural and evil. The flesh loves religion! It gives a false sense of safety and achievement.

Religion makes people feel more holy, with less reason to bow before God in order to be saved. In the process it moves them farther away from God.

Jesus' words show how the flesh can camouflage itself with God's words and miss Him completely. People's false observance of the Sabbath rules reveals how they overlook God's heart. This is the surest proof that the flesh is at work and not the Spirit of God.

Be warned: loyalty towards religion and rules encourages rebellion towards God. Rules multiply the sordid deeds of the flesh and resist God's Spirit. Only loyalty towards the Son of God gives life.

# WORDS REVEAL THE HEART

*"I tell you that everyone will have to give account on the Day of Judgment for every empty word they have spoken."*
Matthew 12:36

The reason for this remark was the reaction of the Pharisees when Jesus saved a demon-possessed man. A delegation had come from Jerusalem to incriminate Jesus, claiming that He was casting out demons through the devil.

Jesus reacted sharply: "You sly people! How do you do it? You pretend to be clerics, but you oppose God. You'll have to give an account to God for your words and unclean hearts from where those words came. Even if you pretend to be holy, God, who sees your hearts, will judge you according to the truth. You can't just do as you please and say what you like. God will demand an account for what you say."

Do your words reveal a pure or an unclean heart? Even if you pretend to be spiritual, God sees what goes on in your heart. Stop your impurity and resistance towards God by bowing before Jesus and asking for forgiveness and cleansing.

# PRIVILEGED EYES

*"Blessed are your eyes because they see, and your ears because they hear."*
Matthew 13:16

How sad that people often only appreciate something when it's gone. We become so used to our blessings that we deal with them recklessly, and are often ungrateful.

Jesus explains that, for many reasons, there are people who can't see the glory of the gospel. They live with God's salvation right in front of them, but they don't share in it. However, His disciples have the privilege of seeing and hearing what God says and does. It's an unspeakable privilege with eternal implications.

Jesus says, "Do you have any idea of what you're part of? Do you know how incredibly fortunate you are? Do you understand that God's blessings rest on you?"

Lord Jesus, may my heart never be dulled by the privilege of having access to God. May this holy privilege refresh my soul every morning when I wake and every evening when I go to sleep. Amen.

# LET IT RISE!

*"The kingdom of heaven is like yeast that a woman took and mixed into about sixty pounds of flour until it worked all through the dough."*
Matthew 13:33

We are familiar with how fast a little yeast permeates a bowl of dough. The kingdom of God is the same: It might seem simple and meaningless, but it can change hearts and conquer the world.

The sovereignty of God draws a person closer and works through their life like yeast, conquering every rebellion and darkness. It spreads from heart to heart and washes like the waves of the sea over land and kingdoms across the universe.

Not even the most fierce opposition or persecution can stop it. You can know for sure that the good work that God has started in you will be completed. Don't resist God's yeast. Let it rise!

Father, let the yeast of Your kingdom permeate my whole life – my finances, my relationships, my words, my actions, my attitude, my dreams and my plans – all of me. Amen.

# AMAZING GRACE

*"'No,' he answered, 'because while you are pulling the weeds, you may uproot the wheat with them. Let both grow together until the harvest. At that time I will tell the harvesters: First collect the weeds and tie them in bundles to be burned; then gather the wheat and bring it into my barn.'"*
Matthew 13:29-30

One often wonders, like David did, why God doesn't just remove all the wicked people and evil in the world. God is absolutely pure and He will punish impurity and wickedness, but He is also completely righteous and merciful – not only towards us, but towards everyone.

There will be a day of reckoning, but there is also definite grace to call all of us – every individual – to repentance. Everyone who embraces God's grace will not only be saved, but also rewarded for the way they serve Him in the face of injustice and evil in the world. Those who reject God's grace will have to give an account before Him for their wickedness, and bear the consequences.

Don't pray for the destruction of wicked people, but rather for their salvation. The day of reckoning will come. Grace is still available now, but when God collects His harvest there will be no more chances.

# GOD-ON-ORDER

*"Why does this generation ask for a sign? Truly I tell you, no sign will be given to it."*
Mark 8:12

The Pharisees' demand for Jesus to give a miraculous sign to prove His authority was basically the same as Satan's requests in the desert. Jesus resisted the devil, and also the Pharisees.

It's as if Jesus is saying, "What! After everything I've done for you and everything I've taught you, you still don't believe? I won't show any such signs. You don't want to believe – you just want to be singled out. I don't play your games. God reveals Himself in abundance every day, but you don't want to see it. You want a God-on-order, not Almighty God."

Jesus was right. Not even His resurrection could persuade them otherwise.

It doesn't help to turn a blind eye towards everything God is doing around us and expect special revelations when we want them.

# EMOTIONALLY DRIVEN OBSTACLES

*"Get behind Me, Satan! You are a stumbling block to Me; you do not have in mind the concerns of God, but merely human concerns."*
Matthew 16:23

Peter didn't expect this reaction from Jesus. He thought he was being loyal in his love for Jesus by trying to prevent His arrest. Jesus' words probably hit him hard. Good intentions are not necessarily right.

Without knowing it, one can prevent God's work in someone's life, while having the best possible intentions. Our emotions get stirred and we act spontaneously – without realizing that we're not thinking the way God expects us to, but rather as humans.

The question should never be about how you feel, but rather "where is God in this matter?" Peter was emotion-driven, not God-driven.

We live in an emotion-fueled world, driven by its statements and actions. Don't allow emotions to lead you. Let God guide you so that you don't become a stumbling block to others.

# SURPRISING DISCOVERIES

*"What do you want Me to do for you?" Jesus asked.*
Mark 10:36

This invitation from Jesus doesn't mean He's going to do everything we ask of Him; rather, it reinforces the revelation of what's going on in our hearts.

The disciples' reaction was quite astonishing. Their request was: "Lord, make us more important than the others." Did Jesus do it? No, but the hidden motives and attitudes of the disciples were definitely revealed!

Most of the time we don't know what's going on in our own hearts. It takes a special event for us to realize this. It's important to know your heart because it determines your actions, words and thoughts. Don't hide your heart. Bring it to the light so that any impurities can be removed.

A disciple of Jesus should be concerned with only one thing: being like Jesus in all things. Anything in their life that is not like Jesus must be removed, not hidden. Ask Jesus to help you with this.

# BAPTIZED WITH SUFFERING

*"You will drink the cup I drink and be baptized with the baptism I am baptized with."*
Mark 10:39

▶ One of Jesus' most important teachings to His disciples is that in this life things will be difficult. Darkness and evil hate the light. In today's Scripture verse, Jesus assures His disciples that they will indeed have to drink from the cup and be baptized with suffering – just like Jesus. This is not a popular teaching, but a very important one.

For the first believers, the gospel didn't mean "come to Jesus and all your troubles will disappear." It meant "come to Jesus and meet Him today." Our extremely self-indulgent culture of materialism easily does away with this truth. Jesus' life in abundance doesn't mean the absence of suffering, but victory in the midst of it!

Be ready to suffer because of Jesus. "Everyone who wants to live a godly life in Christ Jesus will be persecuted" (2 Tim. 3:12). Your faith in Jesus doesn't keep suffering away; it guarantees it.

# SIN WILL BE PUNISHED

*"The Son of Man is going to come in His Father's glory with His angels, and then He will reward each person according to what they have done."*
Matthew 16:27

You won't understand God's grace if you don't understand how much God hates sin. The cross makes no sense if you don't understand the devastation that sin causes. The more the world condones sin, the stranger Jesus' cruel death on the cross and the need for salvation become.

Jesus is not only the Savior who died for the sins of man, but also the Righteous Judge who will judge all people according to their deeds. Sin will always be punished. God punished Jesus in our place so that we could stand before Him with a new life. Everyone who rejects this will have to carry the punishment.

One sometimes wonders why people are so foolish – carrying the punishment of sin when Jesus has done it for us. People do it for the "privilege" of being their own gods instead of standing under God's authority.

# A RUTHLESS ENEMY

*"Neither will I tell you by what authority I am doing these things."*
Mark 11:33

God gives grace to the humble but opposes the proud. This is a message that is illustrated throughout the Bible, as well as in today's Scripture verse.

The Pharisees wanted to play games with Jesus because they were proud and arrogant. Not only did they face social embarrassment, but they also lost the privilege of getting to know Jesus better.

Jesus distanced Himself from them and as a result they remained ignorant. Was it wrong of Jesus to do this? No, because He knew what was going on in their hearts. They had no desire to get to know God, but only to promote themselves at the expense of others. God reveals Himself only to those who search for Him in truth.

The hardhearted become more hardhearted and the wicked become more wicked, but those who search for the Lord in truth will discover the riches of His glory! Stubbornness is not something to brag about – it's a ruthless enemy.

# HONOR YOUR HERO

*"Whoever takes the lowly position of this child is the greatest in the kingdom of heaven."*
Matthew 18:4

▶ This concept is very different to what we're familiar with. Usually we think of ourselves as important and others as insignificant. We even regard our own opinions, plans and dreams as more important than God's. True prominence starts when we renounce our self-worship, and worship God.

Children shamelessly honor their heroes. One sees this on the sports field – fans ask for signatures, collect souvenirs and live for the chance of speaking a few words to the one they idolize. They honor their heroes without holding anything back. Jesus shows His disciples the great secret to success in God's kingdom: Don't try to be your own hero! We already have one.

Worship God like little children. Honor Him without holding back. Everyone who does this is a VIP in God's kingdom.

# FULLY RELY ON GOD

*"How hard it is for the rich to enter the kingdom of God!"*
Mark 10:23

▶ Why is this so? Are the poor stronger from a spiritual perspective? No, it's not more "spiritual" to be poor, but poor people often have fewer things to rely on other than God. Rich people lapse more easily into the delusion that they are self-sufficient and independent. It's easy for them to say that they trust God, when they actually rely on their own resources.

When poor people have to choose between God and their own lives, they choose God because they have nothing left. When rich people have to choose, it's more difficult. They feel that they have to pay a "price" to follow God. For poor people, God is often the great escape, while for the rich, choosing God feels like a loss.

God doesn't care about your bank balance. He cares about the things that people surrender to Him. You don't have to own a lot to do this. Don't allow "things" to rob you of God.

# GOD OF THE IMPOSSIBLE

*"With man this is impossible, but not with God; all things are possible with God."*
*Mark 10:27*

After Jesus' previous words about wealth and the Kingdom, His disciples wanted to know who could be saved. Jesus answers, "It's impossible for you to save someone else – rich or poor. You don't even have to try! God is the expert on matters of the heart. He knows how to deal with people. He works continuously with each person – He can bring them to the truth.

"He can help a person see what they otherwise might have missed. He can do the impossible. He can save people from darkness and bring them into the kingdom of light. Allow God to work in people's lives without interfering."

God is the One who works – we are only His co-workers. Don't run ahead of God – stay in step with Him. He is the God of the impossible.

# LIKE JESUS

*"Whoever wants to become great among you must be your servant, and whoever wants to be first must be slave of all."*
Mark 10:43-44

What does it mean to be a servant? Sometimes people are scared that serving others means to become a "doormat." It is to be like Jesus – He is no one's doormat, but He is a servant (see Matt. 20:28).

Service, however, comes before ministry, which entails giving of yourself. Jesus asks that His disciples set their own interests aside. To serve others is to stand under God's authority.

Ministry itself is easy. It is possible to minister to others and not stand under God's authority. However, it is not possible to serve and not be under God's authority. Service is first of all an attitude of submission to God. That is what is significant to God – not status or rank.

To serve others you must submit to God. What God wants you to do, that you must do (for example, forgiving others when they sin against you). That's the heart of a servant.

# SALT OF THE EARTH

*"Salt is good, but if it loses its saltiness, how can you make it salty again? Have salt among yourselves, and be at peace with each other."*
Mark 9:50

Salt brings out the flavor in food. It also preserves. To be salt to the world means to bring out the best in others and to preserve each other from sin. To be salt is to bring peace and love.

Jesus' disciples are God's salt to the world. They uplift lives and societies because they are submissive.

What will happen if they're no longer submissive? Who will then be the salt? What will happen when they no longer bring out the best in others and keep each other from sin? When salt is not salt anymore, it serves no purpose.

Jesus' reminder is applicable to you today: "You must have the qualities of salt and live in peace with each other."

# THE GLORY AFTERWARD

*"The Son of Man did not come to be served, but to serve, and to give His life as a ransom for many."*
Mark 10:45

Jesus was arrested, untruthfully charged and most unfairly tried; He was tortured, ridiculed, mocked and killed. Humans walked over Him and spat on Him. That's what He got for being a servant of the people! He was a doormat! Or was He? What He did and what He had to endure were not because He was society's doormat, but because He was obedient to God.

To Him it was not important what people thought and said. He walked the road that God had laid out for Him. And why would God want this for His Son? The answer is far greater than we can imagine! Our salvation is the result. Peter talks about "the sufferings of the Messiah and the glories that would follow" (1 Pet. 1:11).

Surrender yourself to God, regardless of what it implies. Look further than what you're going through at present – look at God's plan – the glory afterward! Then everything makes sense.

# THE REASON
# FOR OBEDIENCE

*"Have faith in God."*
Mark 11:22

It is impossible to serve God without having faith in Him. To have faith in God means to believe that He is who He says He is, and that He can do what He says He can. That's the motivation for doing what God says. When times are tough and circumstances far from ideal, you can know for sure that God is faithful and true.

That is the reason why Jesus endured being martyred, why Jesus allowed people to crucify Him.

He did what God wanted Him to do because He had faith in God. He knew that God would resurrect Him, that God would glorify Him and that God always keeps His promises.

Faith in God is the motivation to do His will. It provides the necessary energy and drive that would otherwise be lacking. Know God and, like Jesus, you'll also do as He says.

# PERSPECTIVES ON PRAYER

*"I tell you, whatever you ask for in prayer, believe that you have received it, and it will be yours."*
Mark 11:24

"A red Ferrari, please. Amen." Yes? No! Why not? James explains: "When you ask, you do not receive, because you ask with wrong motives, that you may spend what you get on your pleasures" (James 4:3).

Jesus' words "Have faith in God" (Mark 11:22) precede today's Scripture verse. To have faith in God and to stand under His authority brings a whole new perspective to your prayer life.

You start to see what God sees and what He wants you to see. You start to talk about the things that are important to God, and focus on what He wants. To pray the wrong way is to pray for things that are not important to God.

If you stand under God's authority, seeing what He sees and talking about what is important to Him, there is nothing you'll ask for in prayer that you will not receive. That is essentially what Jesus is saying in today's verse.

# AVOID, DON'T OPPOSE

*"Watch out for the teachers of the law. They like to walk around in flowing robes and be greeted with respect in the marketplaces, and have the most important seats in the synagogues and the places of honor at banquets."*
Mark 12:38-39

Beware of people who put their behavior on display! Such people are only concerned about their own interests and will do anything to get it. They go to extremes when they feel that their "rights" have been violated. They justify any action as long as it suits them – even murder.

Jesus proved it. Self-righteous people are not only a threat to others, but also repulsive in God's sight. God opposes such people (see James 4:6). Jesus' warning is not to stir believers to act against people like this, but rather to avoid them. If any action needs to be taken, God will do it Himself.

Be careful that "they" don't become you. When you start insisting on people's respect and honor, you're in trouble!

# LEADER OR DECEIVER?

*"Be on your guard; I have told you everything ahead of time."*
Mark 13:23

Jesus warned His disciples in advance that there would be people who would try to deceive them. Jesus is our Leader, and anyone else who wants to send believers in another direction is a deceiver.

Jesus says, "Watch out for such people, because they're out there." Believers have only one Leader and one way to go, and that is Jesus.

It is important for believers to be able to distinguish between Jesus' guidance and that of people. Avoid the deceivers at all costs. Even more importantly: Avoid being misled. The most essential thing is to know Jesus' way, to know His voice, His character, His nature and His truth. Without this knowledge everyone will be deceived.

There are many voices and ways in the church today. Watch out! Don't be deceived.

# GLORY AND TERROR

*"At that time people will see the
Son of Man coming in clouds
with great power and glory."*
Mark 13:26

The Second Coming is an event that all believers look forward to. It's something that Christians use to encourage each other (see 1 Thess. 4:18).

The world will not continue in this way forever. The end will come – not the end of life, but the end of injustice and evil. A final revelation is coming of Christ as Judge and King. He will give the final verdict about unrighteousness and end it once and for all.

For believers this is something to look forward to, but for the ungodly it is terrifying. The world says, "Leave us alone!" The church says, "Amen. Come, Lord Jesus!" (Rev. 22:20).

"In just a little while, He who is coming will come and will not delay" (Heb. 10:37). Be ready. "Encourage one another and build each other up, just as in fact you are doing" (1 Thess. 5:11).

# KEEP WATCH!

*"Keep watch because you do not know when the owner of the house will come back – whether in the evening, or at midnight, or when the rooster crows, or at dawn. If he comes suddenly, do not let him find you sleeping. What I say to you, I say to everyone: 'Watch!'"*
Mark 13:35-37

Whether it's the Second Coming or your passing, it will happen quickly and without warning. Only people who are not made right with God want to know when this will happen. It's as if people want to "get ready" when the moment arrives, but in the meantime they want to enjoy life. What is left to enjoy outside of God's will? Sin? Sin tears lives apart and destroys relationships, robbing people of their lives.

Jesus' warning is both loving and timely: "Get ready now! Live a righteous life now, because you don't know when the end will come." The emphasis is not on "getting" ready, but "being" ready. These people are far less concerned about when and more concerned about being ready every day.

Be alert and stay watchful. It's a lifestyle, not a single action. Jesus' words are significant – don't lose sight of this.

# PAY YOUR BILLS!

*"Give back to Caesar what is Caesar's and to God what is God's."*
Mark 12:17

"Give to everyone what belongs to them." That's the clear message. Paul wrote a year later, "Give to everyone what you owe them: If you owe taxes, pay taxes; if revenue, then revenue; if respect, then respect; if honor, then honor" (Rom. 13:7). Pay your bills, pay your fines, pay your taxes, but above all – give your life to God because it belongs to Him.

To withhold that which "belongs to Caesar" is rebellion towards God. To withhold that which belongs to God is rebellion towards Him. Rebellion doesn't bring life, only death. God will repay us for what is due us: life if it is life and death if it is death. Don't make excuses to evade God.

It doesn't matter what other people are doing. You won't be judged on their actions, only your own. Choose to serve God, irrespective of popular beliefs.

# THE EXPERT

*"Put out into deep water, and let down the nets for a catch."*
Luke 5:4

After a whole night on the lake – and an unsuccessful one at that – Jesus asked the hardened and experienced fishermen to go out again. Experience had taught them that in such circumstances the fish wouldn't bite. They knew what they were doing and they knew the lake. Why should they go out again? It was pointless, and they were tired and cold.

Jesus was no fisherman. He was one of the spectators looking on from the shore. Nevertheless, they turned around and did what Jesus asked. Maybe this was because they respected Him and didn't have the courage to oppose Him. Then the surprise! There were so many fish that they had to ask another boat to help them because their nets began to tear.

Whatever you think you know – Jesus knows more! He is the Expert of experts. Listen to Him, even if what He tells you sounds ridiculous and unnecessary.

# BE ON GUARD

*"You must be on your guard."*
Mark 13:9

This is valuable advice! We often hear that we must watch out for other people, but not that we need to watch out for ourselves. The heart of man is deceitful above all things. Our hearts often make us our own worst enemy.

The moment we begin to struggle a little, we find all manner of excuses – even ungodly ones. We argue and rationalize. We justify and make excuses. Be careful! Keep to the truth of God even if it means enduring tough times of persecution. Don't adapt God's truth to suit your own. When popularity and convenience become your highest aspirations, God's truth is often the first to go. Be on guard and be vigilant.

Test yourself all the time to see if you're walking in faith and truth, especially when times are tough. Jesus' warning is not without reason. Don't let your own heart lead you away from God.

# DON'T BE DISCOURAGED

*"Everyone who asks receives; the one who seeks finds; and to the one who knocks, the door will be opened."*
Luke 11:10

In this Scripture verse Jesus is mainly referring to people in a relationship with God, but these words can also be true in other areas.

"If you're looking for trouble, you'll get it!" With these words, teachers threaten learners to try and get them to behave. We often say "he got what he deserved" when the trouble-maker receives a thrashing.

Today's Scripture verse holds a blessing and a warning. The warning is this: "You will reap what you sow. Be careful, then, how you live." As a blessing it says: "God is with you. Talk to Him, for He hears you. He wants to reveal His love to you. Don't be discouraged. Trust Him – He rewards everyone who seeks Him."

Your life is already a beautiful explanation of Jesus' words as a blessing and a warning. Learn from the warning and trust in the promise.

# DON'T BE SHORTSIGHTED

*"Truly I tell you," Jesus continued,
"no prophet is accepted
in his hometown."*
Luke 4:24

There is often much more to people than we think. We get to know someone in a certain way and become blind to the other facets of their personality – often to our own detriment. What prevented the people of Nazareth, the place where Jesus grew up, from accepting the Son of God?

"Is He not the son of the carpenter?" "Is His mother not Mary and His brothers James, Joseph, Simon and Judas?" The people thought they knew Him. "Is He not …?"

Little did they know! What a pity. Their reluctance to acknowledge Jesus for who He was, was not a reflection on Jesus, but on their own shortsightedness. It happens so easily – and it can happen to anyone.

Don't make the same mistake! Don't let poor judgment rob you of receiving a blessing from someone. God wants to bless you. Be open and ready to receive it.

# FAITHFUL UNTO DEATH

*"Abba, Father," Jesus said, "everything is possible for You. Take this cup from Me. Yet not what I will, but what You will."*
Mark 14:36

What a moment! Jesus knew what lay ahead. He knew what the Father wanted. He also knew that obedience to God didn't always imply sunshine and roses.

Jesus knew what was waiting for Him. With much emotion, He cried out to heaven. He admitted His fears, but He didn't allow them to overcome Him. That's the important thing.

To be obedient to God can land us in dire circumstances. It can cause great distress. But are we prepared to say what Jesus said: "Yet not what I will, but what You will"? Jesus relied completely on God, regardless of the consequences. That is true obedience.

Millions of believers all over the world experience similar situations on a daily basis. Pray that they will be faithful like Jesus. Go and do the same.

# THE GREAT TEMPTATION

*"Watch and pray so that you will not fall into temptation. The spirit is willing, but the flesh is weak."*
Mark 14:38

We are tempted to be disobedient to God, especially when obedience holds negative consequences. The only way to avoid this is to have a vigilant spirit and to know God's will. The spirit of a disciple wants to obey God. It's the motivation for our whole existence!

However, the flesh wants to protect itself at all costs, even if it means disobeying God.

Jesus says, "Don't allow the flesh to take the lead! This can happen so easily. Your salvation and blessing lie in obedience to God, not in self protection. Be mindful. There will be times and situations where you'll have to fight against it. Fight at all costs!"

Father, I want to follow in Jesus' footsteps – even when times are tough and when the prospects are bleak. Give me a watchful spirit to stay obedient to You. Amen.

# SEPTEMBER

# THE FINAL SAY

*"My Father, who has given them to Me, is greater than all; no one can snatch them out of My Father's hand."*
John 10:29

Believers have a very special place in God's heart. They are very important to Him. The world has no time for them, but Jesus has all the time in the world for them.

Jesus says, "The world is full of bullies, but they don't have the power to take My people away from Me. My sheep have My full attention. Nothing they do goes unnoticed.

"Anyone who touches them will be held accountable before Me. I will repay each one for the disrespect and abuse towards My sheep, because they belong to Me. I gave My life for them and they will be with Me until the end." This is not just a warning to the world, but a deep comfort for every believer.

To be deemed important in God's eyes is no small matter! It assures us of His presence in our lives and the protection of His righteous judgment. Don't think that the injustices of the world have the final say.

# ROUGH SEAS

*"Everyone will be
salted with fire."*
Mark 9:49

▶ Years ago a man once said to me, "God is not interested in your comfort; He is interested in your character."
This is so true! It's much the same as the saying "smooth
seas do not make skilful sailors."

To be refined means to be made pure. Character is what
helps a person stand when everything is falling down. To
have such a character entails hard work and faithfulness
to God. It is precisely through difficult circumstances and
"rough seas" that we learn to stay faithful to God and do
what He says.

Character that is shaped through tough times is refined
and purified. Of course we want things to always run
smoothly, but then we learn nothing. It takes the fires of
affliction to shape and keep the steadfast character of
Jesus.

Pull your crises closer; don't just push them away. It is these
"enemies," threats and discomfort that give the victory of
character when you stay obedient to God.

# CHOICES

*"If you do not remain in Me, you are like a branch that is thrown away and withers; such branches are picked up, thrown into the fire and burned."*

John 15:6

This comparison confirms the truth of choices and outcomes. The choices that we make, good or bad, have inevitable consequences.

It also explains an important issue about "salvation." To witness about choosing Jesus is wonderful, but it's not the only important thing. To choose Jesus is a continuous action, until the end.

It is possible to choose Jesus, to be saved from the world and sin, and then to reject Him. The emphasis is not on "choosing" Jesus, but "remaining in Him." Jesus encourages believers to remain in Him until the very end and never to wander away from Him. There is no life apart from Him.

It's important to be able to testify about your faith in Christ, but it's even more important to live and stand by it every day. Although no one can snatch me from His hand, I can still choose to let go of Him.

# FAITHFUL UNTIL THE END

*"As the Father has loved Me, so have I loved you. Now remain in My love."*
John 15:9

The message of John 15 is very strong: "Don't only start living in My love – remain in it!" Faithfulness to Jesus is the main focus here, not faultlessness. To remain in Jesus' love is to do what He says – to maintain an attitude of submission to Christ.

Jesus explains in verse 10: "If you keep My commands, you will remain in My love, just as I have kept My Father's commands and remain in His love." To be rebellious towards God is to move away from His love. Grace means that God reaches out to us even when we rebel against Him.

God will, however, judge each person who rejects His mercy and grace. God is gracious and gives grace freely, but we must remain in this grace!

The gospel of Jesus is not just a message of salvation; it is also a message of continued obedience. "Run in such a way as to get the prize," says Paul (1 Cor. 9:24).

# THE REASON FOR GREAT JOY

*"I have told you this so that My joy may be in you and that your joy may be complete."*
John 15:11

Jesus says, "Know this – as long as you remain in My love you will be filled with the power and glory of God. It doesn't matter what happens to you. Your life lies in your relationship with the Father.

"There is great joy in this, because you're guaranteed of victory over the world and the powers of Satan. Nothing that people do will get the better of you – even if you're killed by them you'll still triumph.

"This doesn't make your circumstances any easier, but it does bring joy to your soul, joy that triumphs over your circumstances. The fact that God always wins, and you with Him, is a source of great joy!"

Our joy lies in God's victory. It also lies in Jesus' joy. Regardless of what lay ahead of Him on His way to Golgotha, He knew that God would have the final say.

# THE SAME WAY I HAVE LOVED YOU

*"My command is this: Love each other as I have loved you."*
John 15:12

Jesus' explanation in John 15 is so simple, yet so powerful. "If you do what I say, then you love Me. If you do what I say, you remain in My love. Always be obedient to Me so that you can remain in My love. And this is what I want you to do: Love each other in the same way I have loved you."

Everything that God says, everything that God wants, is summed up in this one command. To embrace this truth is to embrace God. To resist this truth is to resist God. Anything you do that is not done with love, opposes God. Anything that you do out of love and wisdom demonstrates obedience to God.

Love needs a definition and an explanation. How does this love work and what is this love? Jesus explains: "… As I have loved you." Obtain the answer to "how does Jesus love us" and you will find the answer to all your other questions.

# HE WILL GIVE THE ANSWER

*"Whenever you are arrested and brought to trial, do not worry beforehand about what to say. Just say whatever is given you at the time, for it is not you speaking, but the Holy Spirit."*
Mark 13:11

▶ Something interesting happens when the world takes action against the followers of Jesus: The world and the disciples come into contact with God in a miraculous way. Believers don't have to think of clever ways to answer the world – they have the privilege of resting quietly in God, because He will give the answer.

The world, however, will hear from God in a unique way, as He will take the defense. Then the judges and prosecutors will stand before the True Judge of Life. Their testimonies and statements will affect their own case before God. The world might prosecute believers, but the process will be controlled by God.

It is not our clever words and arguments that will hold water with God, but rather our actions in the situation. Follow His advice carefully, and see how He will reveal Himself.

# DO NOT JUDGE

*"Do not judge, and you will not be judged. Do not condemn, and you will not be condemned. Forgive, and you will be forgiven."*
Luke 6:37

No matter how you look at these words, the message is very clear: If you confess your sins of rebellion and lovelessness to God, He will cleanse you.

That's the reason why Jesus died on the cross. But if you refuse to forgive others, that same rebellion will come against you.

There is no explanation that can take this away. Jesus' words are direct and clear. If you think about it, you will understand why Jesus is saying this: How can we claim God's righteousness and redemption for ourselves, but refuse to show it to others? If we think we have this right, we're arrogant and seriously misled.

If we look for arguments or reasons why we don't have to forgive others, we will then also see why God doesn't have to forgive us.

# SPIRITUAL GUIDANCE

*"Can the blind lead the blind? Will they not both fall into a pit?"*
Luke 6:39

The world asks, "Do you have the right theological qualifications?" God asks, "Are your eyes opened?" Unfortunately the answer is not the same for both questions. We can't please the world by answering that our "eyes are open," because people are not interested in this. In the same way we can't answer God's question by saying that, yes, we are qualified, because this is not what interests Him.

A person who has not been made alive by Jesus cannot lead another person in spiritual matters. No amount of theological training or experience in "church work" gives a person this competence. Without the life and character of Christ, we are blind and incompetent to give any kind of spiritual guidance.

Jesus says, "If you are spiritually incompetent and pretend to be a spiritual leader, you and the people you lead will fall into a ditch."

# DON'T GIVE UP!

*"The one who stands firm to the end will be saved."*
Mark 13:13

These words of Jesus are best understood in the face of persecution, which has the ability to discourage people from remaining committed to Him. This only brings trouble, suffering and destruction. Many believers have renounced their faith because of persecution.

This is a big mistake, as there is no life and salvation outside of Jesus. His warning is important.

"God will understand" is no excuse to turn your back on Him. Anyone who does this and teaches others to do the same will be stripped of life. However, the one who endures to the end will be saved.

Don't allow anything, not even death, to pull you away from Jesus. Stay committed to Him, even if it means suffering. God's eternal reward far exceeds anything we have to endure on earth.

# FALSE PROPHETS

*"False messiahs and false
prophets will appear ..."*
Mark 13:22

Jesus' words are never empty. A false messiah and false prophets are not only people pretending to be the real Messiah and true prophets, but also people posing as "alternatives."

There are many alternative messiahs and prophets. They offer a different path from Jesus' way; some other word, gospel and solution.

"Watch out for them," says Jesus, "they quietly rise up, unnoticed. That's why you should know My voice, so that you can distinguish the alternative voices from Mine. They take people by surprise and lead them away from Me. Such people are bearers of death."

Don't fall for things that "sound fine." Listen only for the voice of Jesus. Heed His warning and protect your heart. Wolves in sheep's clothing may look like sheep, but they remain ravenous wolves!

# RUN TO GOD!

*"... and perform signs and wonders to deceive, if possible, even the elect."*
Mark 13:22

▶ There are few things that so easily mislead and confuse people as signs and wonders. Someone once said that if you want to have a church building that is full, just perform a few signs and wonders. People will rush to see it.

Of course God does perform wonders and miracles, but not everyone who performs a miracle is from God. Do you remember Jesus' words? "Many will say to Me on that day, 'Lord, Lord, did we not prophesy in Your name and in Your name drive out demons and in Your name perform many miracles?' Then I will tell them plainly, 'I never knew you. Away from Me, you evildoers!'" (Matt. 7:22-23). Don't run towards wonders and signs, run to God! Again, Jesus' warning is not empty. It was true 2,000 years ago and it's still true today.

God never measures our spirituality against our ability to perform signs and wonders, but against our obedience to His voice. People who perform miracles are not necessarily obedient to God. Don't be deceived.

# JESUS' URGENT WARNING

*"Be on your guard; I have told you everything ahead of time."*
Mark 13:23

Be on guard for what? Be on guard for people posing as servants of God but are not; for people posing as messengers of some other way to God. Stay away, even if they can perform signs and wonders. Why? Because these people's hearts are not with God and their aim is not bringing people to Jesus. If you follow them you will not find Jesus. And if you don't have Jesus, you don't have God.

Be careful. Don't believe everything you hear. Not everything that sounds spiritual and godly is spiritual and godly. This is the biggest danger for believers. It often allows false prophets into the inner circle and brings only destruction and suffering.

Jesus gives two instructions about false messiahs and prophets (and reiterates the urgency thereof). Firstly, Jesus says that we must avoid such people. Secondly, we must remove these people from our midst. Read Revelation 2-3.

# ARE YOU DOING THE SAME?

*"Leave her alone," Jesus replied. "It was intended that she should save this perfume for the day of My burial."*
John 12:7

Mary, Lazarus's sister, once anointed Jesus' feet with very expensive oil. It caused quite an uproar. She was criticized for wasting money because of the way she worshipped and thanked Jesus. Then He said, "Why are you making it difficult for her?" How easily this happens!

We often see significance in the most unimportant things – especially in light of the things that really are important. The bystanders had nothing to say about Mary's love and worship towards Jesus, but they had a lot to say about how she did it.

What did it matter? Instead of making it easy for her to love and serve Jesus, they made life difficult for her with their shortsightedness.

Have you done the same in the past? Are you making it hard for someone to serve and worship Jesus with your senseless arguments and attitude? Don't sweat the small stuff. Focus on Jesus!

# NO GREATER LOVE

*"Greater love has no one than this: to lay down one's life for one's friends."*
John 15:13

One hears this quote from Scripture oftentimes in books and movies (for example in *The Jungle Book*), and then one wonders if the author knows where it actually comes from. Jesus did not only give up His own life for His disciples and us by dying on a cross, but He also laid down a life of service for us.

To lay down your life for someone is the ultimate definition of love. When I see how my wife lays down her life for me, I know that she loves me unconditionally. Love doesn't demand the other person to lay down their life; love gives itself. Love doesn't ask the other person to lay down their lives first – it does so anyway.

"Follow My example!" Jesus calls out. Those who follow Him in this are His followers. Those who refuse are His opposition. Where does this place you?

# MORE THAN A MASTER

*"I no longer call you servants, because a servant does not know his master's business. Instead, I have called you friends, for everything that I learned from My Father I have made known to you."*
John 15:15

Although Jesus is the only true Lord and asks complete obedience of us, His relationship with us is so much more than that of a master and slave.

It is a relationship of love. Jesus trusts us and reveals Himself to us. He shares His plans and His heart with us and invites us to share our hearts with Him.

He is interested in us. He is involved in our lives and spends time with us. He wants to share everything with us. This is so much more than just a master. Jesus doesn't hold anything back. He invites us to do the same.

The privilege of a relationship with Jesus is indescribable. He gives us full access to the glory and love of God. That is our greatest wealth.

# YOU COULD BE A JUDAS TOO

*"Truly I tell you, one of you will betray Me – one who is eating with Me."*
Mark 14:18

▶ Judas is synonymous with betrayal. If we say someone is a Judas, the meaning behind the words is quite clear. Judas did betray Jesus, but there is another important thing to remember here: Judas was also a disciple. He ate with Jesus. He was counted amongst those who sided with Him. He was in the "praise and worship band" and He taught Sunday school class. Judas was an elder and a minister, the chairman of the financial committee. He did missionary work with Jesus and was part of the Bible study group.

That is what makes Judas a terror – because it could be you or the person sitting next to you. How would you know? Accordingly, if you think you are standing strong, be careful not to fall (see 1 Cor. 10:12).

The pretense of people often masks what is really going on in their hearts. Be careful of what you allow into your heart. You could also offend Jesus, and be someone who betrays Him – it wasn't only Judas.

# AVOID THE WOLVES

*"Watch out for false prophets. They come to you in sheep's clothing, but inwardly they are ferocious wolves."*
Matthew 7:15

A false prophet is someone who claims to speak the words of God, but doesn't. It's someone who pretends that God sent them when He didn't. Why would someone do that? Precisely! How would someone do this? The answer is very sinister. A person like this maintains a shady tactic to hide their true colors. Their true nature is that of a devouring wolf, but they pretend to be an innocent little lamb.

These people are dangerous and have a dangerous agenda. Jesus says, "Beware of them! Avoid them at all costs. They are not lambs; they are wolves that want to devour you any chance they get."

Not everyone who says "Lord, Lord" is a disciple of Jesus. And not everyone who says, "Thus says the Lord" is speaking the truth. Don't be ignorant and naïve – it can lead to great danger.

# CHOOSE WISELY

*"Whoever acknowledges Me before others, I will also acknowledge before My Father in heaven."*
Matthew 10:32

That's easy, isn't it? No, not really. Jesus represents everything the world hates. His name is a popular swear word for good reason. He was not extradited and murdered and His followers martyred and slain for nothing.

To identify yourself with Jesus could be one of your biggest social blunders. However, you need to choose wisely. Deny Jesus and enjoy the respect of people – even important people; or identify yourself openly with Jesus and enjoy the respect and recognition of God. Whatever you choose will dramatically and deeply influence your life. Choose wisely and carefully, and prepare yourself for the inevitable consequences – whatever choice you make.

If you consider that all people will stand before the judgment seat of God and give account for their lives, it's silly to choose people over the Judge.

# KNOW THE DIFFERENCE!

*"The Advocate, the Holy Spirit, whom the Father will send in My name, will teach you all things and will remind you of everything I have said to you."*
John 14:26

▶ The ministry of the Holy Spirit is so precious! Unfortunately, some people have a distorted view of who the Holy Spirit is and what He does. Because of that, they are scared of Him.

Jesus explains it well: "The Holy Spirit's task is to teach you more about Me. Nothing else. That is how you will know that the Spirit is with you and works among you.

"You'll start to see Me more clearly. The Holy Spirit doesn't draw attention to Himself, but focuses all the attention on Me. Don't let people fool you. The Holy Spirit's main focus is not gifts and manifestations, but to reveal more of Me. Never lose sight of this truth!"

If gifts and manifestations don't emphasize Jesus, it's not the work of the Holy Spirit. Due to our humanity, however, we do love gifts and manifestations. Know the difference!

# THE HOUSE OF THE LORD

*"Destroy this temple, and I will raise it again in three days."*
John 2:19

I grew up with this phrase: "Welcome to the house of the Lord." It was the customary words of welcome at church services on Sundays.

Years later I wondered how the church leaders managed to greet us in this way! Even today, many people don't understand it. No building, however beautiful, is "the house of the Lord."

It was true of the temple in Jerusalem, but it's no longer true of any building on earth. Jesus established a new temple – a new dwelling place for God. That temple is the body of Christ. He is present in His people. The dwelling place of God is wherever the body of Christ is.

The temple of God is in people – not in systems or buildings. Take note of the way you talk, and correct yourself according to Jesus' truth.

# WITH EVERYTHING THEY HAVE

*"Blessed are the poor in spirit, for theirs is the kingdom of heaven."*
Matthew 5:3

People who know how dependent they are on God live in and from His truth. This is more than simply trusting God for rain for crops. It is to acknowledge that any and all salvation and truth come from God and God alone.

Truth is not determined by your culture, preferences or fashion of the day. It is found only in God. It is to know how dependent we are on God and to look for life and truth in Him and nowhere else. The kingdom of God belongs to such people. They embrace Jesus with everything they have.

It's easy to identify someone who understands their dependence of God. Such a person holds unwaveringly onto God in everything.

# BE TRULY GLAD

*"Rejoice and be glad, because
great is your reward in heaven, for
in the same way they persecuted the
prophets who were before you."*
Matthew 5:12

Persecution is not a natural source of joy. Soft music is not playing in the background when someone persecutes you. It is dreadful! Yet the same reason you rejoice is also the reason why you may be persecuted.

If you're persecuted because you're a criminal, there is no reason for joy. But when you're persecuted because of Christ, the reason for your joy should be overwhelming. Persecution because of Christ means the world acknowledges you as being associated with Jesus, God's loving Son. That's the mark of recognition that you don't stand under the rule of Satan, but are committed to God. That's great joy!

Jesus' explanation brings perspective and comfort. To see things like God sees them brings so much clarity. Rejoice in it!

# GO THE EXTRA MILE

*"If anyone forces you to go one mile, go with them two miles."*
Matthew 5:41

▶ According to regulations in biblical times, Roman soldiers had permission to force any male Jew to carry their load for them for about one kilometer. Jesus' words bring a surprising perspective to the Romans' oppression of the Jews.

Jesus says, "You are better than this. If an oppressor forces you to carry his baggage for one kilometer, carry it for two kilometers out of your own free will. Surprise him with the character of God by serving him – even if it's unreasonable. In any case, you don't stand under the authority of people – you're under God's authority. Don't worry that your actions will be interpreted as weakness. Serve God! No one is stronger than He!"

To stand under God's authority brings wonderful freedom and the ability to act surprisingly differently. We are not dominated by people or circumstances – we serve God.

# DON'T TURN AWAY

*"Give to the one who asks you, and do not turn away from the one who wants to borrow from you."*
Matthew 5:42

"Be accommodating." That's a most important characteristic. Jesus' words are justified when He says, "In this way, you will be acting as true children of your Father in heaven. He gives His sunlight to both the evil and the good, and He sends rain on the just and the unjust alike" (see v. 45). After all, that's how He reached us!

Don't lend and borrow unwisely, but be available to help people in need. Don't be insensitive towards people. It's easy to become unsympathetic to others' needs when you're bombarded by them daily or caught out by people's tricks. To keep your heart and spirit sensitive requires practice, but God will help you.

Insensitivity is often a mechanism of self protection, but it's something that should not be a characteristic of Jesus' followers. Rather arm yourself with the character of God, which promises life and joy.

# THE MOTHER OF ALL FEARS

*"You of little faith, why are you so afraid?"*
Matthew 8:26

Jesus' objection is not against the disciples' fear of the storm, but rather against their fear that God would forsake them. Many situations scare us because they are terrifying.

The circumstances leading up to His crucifixion scared Jesus, but His fear was never that God would forsake Him – even in death. The fact that Jesus says the disciples have "so little faith" is indicative of this.

Yes, the storm is terrifying, but God will never forsake His children, no matter what. That's the one thing children of God never have to fear. In fact, it is this knowledge that dispels all other fears.

The fear that God will forsake you is the "mother" of all fears. And it's the one fear without any good reason. Jesus had a purpose in asking the disciples why they were afraid, since God will never leave us or forsake us.

# THE SONG OF LIFE

*"Take heart, daughter," He said,
"your faith has healed you."*
Matthew 9:22

This is another example of the kind of faith that Jesus is after. It's not just faith that Jesus will hear, but the belief that He is in fact the true Christ.

This woman's faith doesn't just unlock the door for Jesus' work in her body, but also in her soul. "Take heart" means the same as "peace be with you" in this case.

There is peace and healing for every person who acknowledges Jesus as the Christ. It would've been tragic if the woman only saw Jesus as the Miracle Healer – yet she didn't. Because of this she received healing from Jesus in her body and in her soul. "How great Thou art" becomes the song of her life.

Faith in Jesus is the best outcome for people. It makes an "impersonal" God very personal and real to us. This woman experienced God in every facet of her life – far greater than she could have imagined.

# ACCESS FOR ALL

*"As you go, proclaim this message:*
*'The kingdom of heaven has*
*come near.'"*
Matthew 10:7

My grandmother always told the story of how, many years ago, her family slept in front of the stadium gates before a big rugby match to make sure they got tickets to watch the Springboks play against New Zealand.

Jesus says, "Tell the people that the gates are open and the tickets available! The kingdom of God is open for all. The waiting is over. As many people as possible can enter because there is room for everyone!"

Share in God's victory over death and darkness! This is far better than a rugby game. God has come close to us and the privilege of being part of God's family is available to all!

Each individual can be part of God's rule. We no longer have to be slaves to sin and to Satan. We can be children of God and He can be our Father.

# THAT EXTRA HOUR

*"Simon, are you asleep? Couldn't you keep watch for one hour?"*
Mark 14:37

Paul challenges believers by saying, "Carry each other's burdens, and in this way you will fulfill the law of Christ" (Gal. 6:2). This is probably one of the most difficult things to do, as Peter found out in Gethsemane.

To stand watch with someone for something that is important to them is not easy. We have enough concerns of our own that drain our energy and deplete our limited resources. For most people, helping others carry their burdens is just a step too far.

However, love is seen in the things that we do that are not easy or comfortable. Accordingly, to share each other's burdens is to fulfill the law of Christ.

To love someone means to look beyond your own interests and concerns. Jesus taught His disciples to love others by walking the extra mile with them and staying awake just one more hour.

# TO DENY HIM

*"Whoever disowns Me before others, I will disown before My Father in heaven."*
Matthew 10:33

Recognition is the biggest driving force in life. It's the greatest motivation for the highest achievement. We can work for years for the recognition of people, and when we receive it we feel successful and established. It's surprising to hear that our recognition (or denial) of Jesus before people has such far-reaching consequences before God.

When we deny Jesus, it similarly results in Him saying, "Father, I don't know this person. They are not part of Us." When we don't side with Jesus or when we're ashamed of Him, when we desire the recognition of people to such an extent that we distance ourselves from Him, He won't side with us and will also be ashamed of us.

Can Jesus distance Himself from us? Yes, He can and He will, depending on your interaction with Him. He is the Shepherd of those who truly want Him to be their Guide.

# OCTOBER

# THE GREATEST PUNISHMENT

*"My God, My God, why have You forsaken Me?"*
Matthew 27:46

I thought God would never abandon us. I thought God loved His Son. Why did Jesus ask this question? The answer is because this is the punishment that He had to carry for you and me.

The suffering and crucifixion are nothing compared to the feeling that God has turned His back on you. That is the punishment and judgment of sin.

It is what Jesus had to endure to pay the full price for our rebellion against God. Never has Jesus been separated from God; never has God rebelled against Jesus. But when the Father placed the sin of the world on Jesus, this was the result.

Rejected by the people, tortured by Satan and abandoned by God – how great the price that You had to pay, Lord! And all of that for my salvation. How great Thou art, Lord, and how eternally You love me. Amen.

# A SNAKE!

*"You brood of vipers, how can you who are evil say anything good? For the mouth speaks what the heart is full of."*
Matthew 12:34

A snake can be cunning and poisonous, sometimes quietly waiting for his prey to be on top of him before he strikes. Some snakes pretend to be dead or harmless as part of their strategy to administer their poison.

Jesus knew that the hearts of the Pharisees were evil, but still they posed as wise and righteous men. Through their pretense they came close enough to people's hearts to poison them with Satan's deadly lies.

When someone shouts, "Snake!" everyone is startled. That's what Jesus was doing: He exposed the Pharisees for who they really were, and their actions against Jesus later on confirmed this.

Jesus warns His followers to be cautious like a snake, but not to actually be a snake. Snakes are filled with poison, while believers' hearts are filled with life. Be very careful of snake-like people.

# THE WORK IS COMPLETE

*Jesus said, "It is finished."*
John 19:30

▶ Like a hot knife through butter, these words cleave through the history of the earth and the existence of man. It was the biggest announcement in human history. "It is finished." The price for our sins is paid. The way to God is open and the new nation of God is ready to be born.

Jesus says that the kingdom of God has come and light has finally overcome the dark. Humanity has been freed from sin and Satan and God's judgment.

There is nothing more that needs to be done – the work is complete. Soon the whole world will see that life triumphs over death for all eternity. Happily, it is available to one and all.

Why would someone reject this work of God? The answer is proof of people's foolishness. Complete salvation and reconciliation are freely available from Jesus. Don't waste this opportunity.

# GOD'S SECRETS

*"The knowledge of the secrets of the kingdom of heaven has been given to you, but not to them."*
Matthew 13:11

The secret to God's kingdom is not accessible to those who do not belong to Jesus; but to believers, the heart of God is revealed.

The world has an interest in the "secrets" of God's kingdom. They publish books about it as guidelines to success – yet they remove Jesus from the secrets. In this way they make Him weak and nothing more than a wonderful ideal.

Conversely, disciples learn the secrets of God and His power because Jesus gives it to them. The mysteries of God become the thrill of their lives! Even the smallest secrets have a great impact on their lives, marriages, character development and calling.

Jesus is the key to the glory of God and a successful life. Even the poor and most insignificant people can share in this, and their lives rewarded with glory and honor.

# PART OF THE FAMILY

*"I am ascending to My Father and your Father, to My God and your God."*
John 20:17

God's plan was not only to forgive people, but to include them in His family. The beauty of the gospel is summed up in one word: "We." In John 17, Jesus prayed: "I have given them the glory that You gave Me, that they may be one as We are one" (v. 22).

Again Jesus says, "Anyone who loves Me will obey My teaching. My Father will love them, and We will come to them and make Our home with them" (John 14:23). Through Jesus, God makes us part of His family. Then we can share in His "We" – counted with the Father and the Son.

Jesus was excluded by God so that we could be included. When God talks about you, He talks about "Us" – a privilege that came at a high price. That's the one thing no one can take away from you.

# A FUTILE EXERCISE

*"Peace I leave with you; My peace I give you. I do not give to you as the world gives. Do not let your hearts be troubled and do not be afraid."*
John 14:27

▶ The world gives peace based on the securities of the world. Money, success, power and materialism are all sources of worldly peace. Advertisements on radio and TV depend on these values.

Jesus' peace is different from this. Even when everything the world strives for is lacking, Jesus' followers still experience peace – even in the midst of tough times. Believers experience peace because the King of peace is with them, even in death. Their peace flows from the fact that Jesus is in control and reigns supreme.

Paul explains: "For Your sake we face death; we are considered as sheep to be slaughtered … Nothing will be able to separate us from the love of God that is in Christ Jesus our Lord" (read Rom. 8:35-39).

Disciples who look for peace in worldly things forfeit the peace and joy that Jesus brings. Their stress levels soar. Don't pursue this futile worldly exercise – receive Jesus' peace.

# FREE WILL

*"I will not say much more to you, for the prince of this world is coming. He has no hold over Me."*

John 14:30

▶ The ruler of this world is Satan. He rules over the world and its systems. Jesus is speaking here in view of His arrest and crucifixion. But how is it then that Jesus says, "He has no power over Me"? Did Satan not arrest, torture and murder Him?

Satan did, but not because he had any power over Jesus. It was all part of God's plan.

Concerning His life, Jesus explains: "No one takes it from Me, but I lay it down of My own accord. I have authority to lay it down and authority to take it up again. This command I received from My Father" (John 10:18).

This statement makes Jesus' offering so much more incredible. Everything He had to endure to pay the price on our behalf Jesus did voluntarily. He could've backed out at any time, but He didn't. He didn't want to.

# STUMBLING BLOCKS

*"Woe to the world because of the things that cause people to stumble! Such things must come, but woe to the person through whom they come!"*
Matthew 18:7

There is never a shortage of stumbling blocks in life, but woe betide the person who acts as a stumbling block. The stumbling blocks that Jesus is talking about here are those people who turn others away from Him with their words, deeds or lives. Paul warns believers to be careful that their lives don't cause others to stumble (see 1 Cor. 8:9).

To the other believers in Rome he wrote: "Let us stop passing judgment on one another. Instead, make up your mind not to put any stumbling block or obstacle in the way of a brother or sister" (Rom. 14:13).

There will always be stumbling blocks, but make sure you aren't one of them! Whatever may cause others to stumble in sin, get rid of it – no matter how harmless it might seem.

Jesus says it is better to have a large millstone tied around your neck and to be drowned in the depths of the sea than to cause another person to stumble in faith (see Mark 9:42). Don't make your freedom in Christ a stumbling block to others.

# MORE THAN WILLING

*"I have authority to lay it down and authority to take it up again. This command I received from My Father."*
John 10:18

In this Scripture verse I hear the Father say, "My Son, it is time to pay the price for sin so that We can be reconciled with people. I'm going to send You to earth as a human to dwell among the people of the earth.

"Then, at the right time, they will arrest You, torture You and kill You. You must carry the sins of the world in order to pay for them, but the process is in My hands. You can withdraw at any time – You don't have to endure it. You can choose what You want to bear, but in order to pay the price in full, You must obey. This means that You will have to die. Decide how far You want to go."

Jesus became flesh out of His own free will. He willingly subjected Himself to people. He knowingly accepted His arrest and endured suffering. He willingly opened His arms to be crucified and He died willingly for us.

# STAND FIRM

*"I give them eternal life, and they shall never perish; no one will snatch them out of My hand."*
John 10:28

▶ God's dedication to everyone who believes in Jesus is absolute. His protection over them is the same. It doesn't mean that nothing bad will ever happen to them – on the contrary! Jesus often warned His disciples that they would have to face difficulties and even death.

However, no one would ever be able to separate them from Him. God will make sure of that.

This doesn't mean that believers will never choose to forsake God. They may, but as long as they choose to be with God, He will take care of them for all eternity. No outsiders will be able to influence this relationship.

When a marriage ends I often hear people say, "That woman ended my marriage." But that's not true. It wasn't "that woman," but rather the spouse. No outsider can break up a relationship when the inside parties stand firm.

# JESUS' PRESENCE

*"Where two or three gather in My name, there am I with them."*
Matthew 18:20

The context of Jesus' words is love, relationships and reconciliation. What He is actually saying is: "Where two or three gather together for reconciliation, I am there among them."

I've attended many gatherings of believers "in the name of Jesus" where He was nowhere to be seen because of selfishness, jealousy and bitterness. When believers' hearts are not united, Jesus is absent. But when believers gather in atonement, love and forgiveness, the glory of Jesus is greatly revealed! That's the reason Jesus came to earth – to reconcile us with the Father and with each other. It's this atonement that demonstrates the power of Jesus.

Carefully read Jesus' words in Matthew 18. Do you apply them to your life? If not, start today. Do what Jesus says and you will experience His power and presence like never before.

# ALWAYS FORGIVE

*"I tell you, not seven times, but
seventy-seven times."*
Matthew 18:22

Peter, in all sincerity, wanted to know how many times one must forgive another – seven times? It's noble to want to forgive someone seven times. It's also appealing, because there is a boundary. If the person trespasses more than seven times, maybe you don't have to forgive them anymore and your bitterness can be justified.

Jesus understood this and surprised Peter with His answer: "Peter, if you follow Me, you will never stop forgiving. There is never a reason for bitterness. Bitterness is sin, which can never be excused or justified. To follow Me means to always forgive everyone for everything. God is the Judge who will punish injustice – yours too if you don't forgive."

If you struggle to forgive, you also struggle to obey God. This requires confession, not excuses. People's acts and deeds that are not performed out of love stand between them and God, but so does bitterness. Get serious about forgiving.

# NO BIGGER DEBT

*"The servant's master took pity on him, canceled the debt and let him go."*
Matthew 18:27

After Jesus had told Peter to always forgive others, He told a story of a man who owed a king a great deal of money.

He couldn't pay his debt so the master ordered him to be sold as a slave along with his family. The man begged the king for mercy, and the master was filled with pity for the man and forgave his debt.

That's what God does with us. Our rebellion towards God is our debt. Our payment is death, and eternity separated from Him. There is no bigger debt than this. "We were by nature deserving of wrath" (Eph. 2:3), but through Jesus all our debts have been paid in full.

You will never be able to repay your debt to God, but Jesus paid it for you. God delivered you from all sin and debt. That is the biggest relief and joy for the soul. Because of this you can live an abundant life.

# WHAT GOES AROUND

*"Shouldn't you have had mercy on your fellow servant just as I had on you?"*
Matthew 18:33

▶ In Jesus' story, a man owed the king a great sum of money, but was released from his debt. This same man had his fellow servant arrested and put in prison until he could pay his debt to him in full.

The king heard about it, called the man and asked him the glaring question: "Shouldn't you also have released him?" The answer is clear: "Of course you should have!" Sadly, the man didn't and the story ends tragically.

The purpose of Jesus' parable is clear: Believers have received everything from God – complete exemption of their debt before God. They have no other choice but to treat others in the same way and forgive them.

The reason why we should live in complete forgiveness is because we've received complete forgiveness from God. The phrase "shouldn't you have?" makes it clear. Are there still people in your life that need your forgiveness?

# LIVE BY GRACE

*"This is how My heavenly Father will treat each of you unless you forgive your brother or sister from your heart."*
Matthew 18:35

We've touched on this topic before, but it's important to hear Jesus' thoughts on it again. How will the Father react when we don't forgive our fellow man? He will do what the king did with the guilty man from Jesus' parable. What did he do? He sent the man to prison to be tortured.

Would a loving God do this? Maybe we should ask, "Will people who are subject to God's authority refuse to forgive others?"

Yes, God will do it, because anyone who refuses to forgive also refuses to stand under God's authority. How can we live by God's grace but refuse to have mercy on others?

Forgiveness is not just a good idea – it's a direct command from God. It's not a luxury, but a necessity. To live in God's grace is to live a life of grace.

# OUR SINFUL NATURE

*"If you want to enter life, keep the commandments."*
Matthew 19:17

Jesus says, "If you want a life that pleases God, you must do what He says." Then we realize how important Jesus is. Anyone who tries to do God's will quickly discovers that it's difficult for our sinful natures to submit to Him, making it impossible to receive God's eternal life.

It is for this reason that Jesus came to earth – to deliver us from human nature so that we could follow God's commands.

Jesus makes it possible for us to receive eternal life. Peter writes, "His divine power has given us everything we need for a godly life" (2 Pet. 1:3). God's authority brings people life.

Jesus' disciples are disciples because they do what He says. Without it they are just walking after Him. Embrace life by submitting to God's authority.

# THE MOST ZEALOUS WITNESS

*"You will receive power when the Holy Spirit comes on you; and you will be My witnesses in Jerusalem, and in all Judea and Samaria, and to the ends of the earth."*
Acts 1:8

▶ The truth of Jesus will not be stopped, not even if Satan sends the worst fires from hell! The gospel will move like the waves of the sea over the whole earth. But, knowing that Satan will try everything to put a stop to it, Jesus' followers need power beyond human ability.

That power comes from the Holy Spirit. When the Holy Spirit comes upon you, you become a bold witness for Jesus, even when your life is threatened.

The church cannot function without the power of the Holy Spirit. Where Jesus' followers are present, the testimony of Jesus is alive and active. The Holy Spirit is the most zealous Witness ever!

I don't know what your understanding of being anointed by the Holy Spirit is, but I pray that you have Jesus' understanding. Without His power, life will be hard for you.

# FIRSTHAND EXPERIENCE

*"Now My soul is troubled."*
John 12:27

The Hebrew writer said, "We do not have a high priest who is unable to empathize with our weaknesses, but we have one who has been tempted in every way, just as we are – yet He did not sin" (Heb. 4:15).

One doesn't always realize what this entails. Sometimes people think we just hang around here on earth while Jesus sits in a perfect heaven saying things we can never apply practically.

That's not true. Jesus understands completely what it means to be human. He knows the joys and moments of fulfillment, but He also knows sadness, stress and devastation. He experienced it all firsthand.

The Jesus in front of you today knows everything you may go through. He knows your fears, heartaches, worries and insecurities. He experienced them firsthand. Trust Him to lead you through them – He knows how.

# SATAN'S DESTRUCTION, GOD'S VICTORY

*"I, when I am lifted up from the earth, will draw all people to Myself."*
John 12:32

Satan planned the crucifixion to destroy Jesus, but God had other plans. When Satan lifted Jesus up to be nailed to the cross, God had another kind of exaltation in place.

Satan's destruction of Jesus was God's victory through Him. The devil raised Jesus up to humiliate and destroy Him, but God used it to give Him a name above all names and before whom every knee will bow and every tongue confess that He is Lord.

Not only was Jesus not destroyed, but He became the beacon of hope that draws people to Him. That which Satan tried to prevent is exactly what took place.

If God says He makes everything work together for the good of those who love Him (see Rom. 8:28), He means it. It doesn't matter what Satan plots against you. Stay close to the Father – He will turn things around for you.

# AN IMPORTANT DECISION

*"Many who are first will be last, and many who are last will be first."*
Matthew 19:30

▶ Because the world and God have two different value systems, Jesus' words in today's Scripture verse are obvious. What is popular with the one is not with the other. What is important to the one is unimportant to the other. Many people who are influential in the eyes of the world are not so significant to God, and many people who are disrespected by the world are VIPs in God's eyes.

To be important to the secular world, you must act like the world, but to be counted with God you must do as He does. The one is north and the other is south. The big question is: Who do you want to be respected by? You can't follow both systems – you'll love the one and hate the other.

Your choice will influence your whole life and determine the end result. We call it a value system because it's all about what is really important to you. Where your heart is, there your treasure will also be.

# NO REASON TO SIN

*"Be careful to do everything they tell you. But do not do what they do, for they do not practice what they preach."*
Matthew 23:3

How insightful! Have you ever met people who proclaim the words of Jesus but don't practice them? Jesus says, "Even though these people are not obedient to God, the words they speak are still God's words. Embrace His words, but don't follow their example. It doesn't help to be disappointed in people like this but then also not follow God's will. They will have to answer to God for their lives – just like you."

It often happens that you get hurt in the church and then reject God. This solves nothing. It makes you just as guilty as the people who hurt you. The sin of others is never a reason to sin yourself.

Acknowledge God's Word, even if it comes through someone who is not committed to Him. Followers of God seek His truth at all times.

# "DO AS I SAY"

*"They tie up heavy, cumbersome loads and put them on other people's shoulders, but they themselves are not willing to lift a finger to move them."*
Matthew 23:4

▶ We've previously compared the Pharisees' religious perspectives with legalism – the dead, human religion that cannot grant life. In today's Scripture verse, Jesus emphasizes one of legalism's characteristics: the fact that it is designed to burden people with a heavy load that is not from God.

The "teachers of the law" like to put this burden on others' shoulders, but they themselves don't bother about it. It is the typical "do as I say, not do as I do" mentality. This is not the way Jesus thinks and acts. His words and teachings bring salvation and deliverance, including freedom from legalism. He doesn't teach anything He does not practice Himself. "Follow Me" is His distinctive characteristic.

Stay away from legalism. Don't allow those who promote it to enslave your conscience. Move in under Jesus' authority and serve Him in freedom and truth!

# TRUE MOTIVES

*"Everything they do is done*
*for people to see."*
Matthew 23:5

We can divide people into two groups: one group wants to please God, while the other wants to please people. The first group desires God's honor, while the second group does everything to gain glory from people. Such people will follow and imitate others as long as they gain approval.

Jesus said that the Pharisees did everything for show. He, however, teaches His disciples to please God and to do everything for Him alone. Above all, Jesus says, we are to do it "in secret."

"Then your Father, who sees what is done in secret, will reward you" (Matt. 6:4). If you do good deeds for show, you'll quickly stop when it loses its appeal. God's children show goodwill because that's who they are – followers imitating the Father.

Someone who wants to be "seen" by others is like a boat at sea without an anchor. Such a person's life is tossed by the waves of people's whims and tendencies. Jesus' anchor, however, is obedience to God, regardless of what people say.

# THE FATHER OF FATHERS

*"Do not call anyone on earth 'father,' for you have one Father, and He is in heaven."*
Matthew 23:9

Jesus is not against the loving reverence and respect for our earthly fathers; in fact He encourages it. The crux of Jesus' message here is when we honor people (including our own fathers) in a way that replaces God as Father.

This happens when your honor and admiration of someone is so strong that you follow him or her even when they do things that are not in line with God's will. No father can demand respect if it goes against God, because God is our heavenly Father.

Respect for God is far more important than respect for people. This is not only relevant for fathers, but for teachers, national heroes, religious leaders and others.

Don't worry about refusing to comply when someone demands something from you that is contrary to the will of God. To honor God above all things is the most honorable and loving thing to do.

# YOUR RESPONSIBILITY

*"Watch out that no one deceives you."*
Matthew 24:4

Deception is very common in today's world and it's found everywhere – even in the church. Jesus gives us the responsibility of making sure we are not deceived. Deceivers can be very sly and sometimes even sincere, but it remains our responsibility not to be misled.

Our true destination is the bosom of the Father through Jesus Christ. Anything or anyone who doesn't help us reach that destination deceives us. Don't allow this to happen.

How do we achieve this? Get to know Jesus' voice. Get to know His character. Spend time with Him and allow Him to shape you. Learn the Word; read and meditate on it. God will never go against His own word.

Be expectant like the people in Berea (see Acts 17:10-11) – have an open mind and be willing to listen to what ministers say, but examine the Scriptures to check that what you're taught is true. Ultimately, it's your responsibility.

# BE READY

*"About that day or hour no one
knows, not even the angels in
heaven, nor the Son, but
only the Father."*
Matthew 24:36

Two things stand out about this verse. Firstly, stop predicting the Second Coming. It's not a sign of spirituality, but of ignorance and even arrogance. When you start predicting Jesus' coming, it suggests that He doesn't know what He's talking about. Secondly, it's not important when He returns, but that it will happen and that it can happen at any time.

To know is not important, but to be ready is. Why do people want to know when Jesus will return? Is it to get ready just before He comes and in the meantime enjoy a life of sin? Thousands of people die every day, most of whom didn't expect it. If they wait for even one day to get their matters with God in order, it could be too late.

Why do people postpone getting their affairs with God in order? What are the things that are so important that people hesitate to be made right with God? Don't delay, make right with God today.

# THE LIGHT IS NOT A TRAIN

*"Then the King will say to those on His right, 'Come, you who are blessed by My Father; take your inheritance, the kingdom prepared for you since the creation of the world.'"*

Matthew 25:34

The gospel of Jesus has a distinctive "here and now" and a "then and there" feature. When we are born again, we receive the kingdom of God "here and now," but at the Second Coming we will take possession of it "then and there."

The work of Christ has a past, a present and a future. He concluded His work on the cross (past), He carries it out through us (present), and with the Second Coming it will be revealed for a final time (future).

Because Jesus died on the cross, we are able to be part of God's salvation. Because we share in His salvation, we can look forward to an eternity with God. Sharing in Him now is a guarantee of being part of the future.

The light in the tunnel for the disciples is not a train; it's the Second Coming and revelation of Jesus!

# AN OPPORTUNITY TO WORSHIP

*"I was hungry and you gave Me something to eat, I was thirsty and you gave Me something to drink, I was a stranger and you invited Me in, I needed clothes and you clothed Me, I was sick and you looked after Me, I was in prison and you came to visit Me."*
Matthew 25:35-36

This is one of the most powerful explanations of what it means to worship and serve God. We can't separate our worship for God from our actions towards people. We can't worship God but distance ourselves from what's happening around us. True worshippers are involved in the needs and wants of the world – especially the necessities of fellow believers. People can see our regard for God in our care for the needy.

That's what love is: It is not indifferent. In the Bible, John encourages believers by saying, "Dear friends, let us love one another, for love comes from God. Everyone who loves has been born of God and knows God" (1 John 4:7).

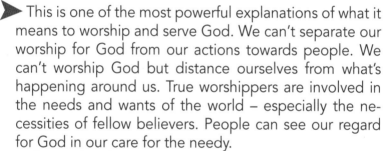

Worship God like Jesus says we should. Ask Him to open your eyes to every opportunity of worship today, and the wisdom to see it through.

# NO SMALL MATTER

*"The King will reply, 'Truly I tell you, whatever you did for one of the least of these brothers and sisters of Mine, you did for Me.'"*
Matthew 25:40

Obedience to God brings one into close contact with people. The less obedient we are to God, the less we bother with those around us. Our worship and obedience to God, however, can be observed and measured according to how we treat "the least among us."

The world has no time for those who are poor, underprivileged or needy, often making excuses for its lack of love towards such people. Jesus says something completely different: His tool for measuring who is the least is very different from how the world "rates" people.

Paul writes, "God chose the lowly things of this world and the despised things – and the things that are not – to nullify the things that are" (1 Cor. 1:28). Do you want to follow Jesus and serve others? Serve the "least" among you, because then you are doing it for God.

Knowledge of God opens your eyes to how important people are. Believers who really know God don't walk over others, especially not those who are vulnerable and lowly.

# A PLENTIFUL HARVEST

*"Very truly I tell you, unless a kernel of wheat falls to the ground and dies, it remains only a single seed."*
John 12:24

▶ Jesus is referring to Himself here. The disciples loved and worshipped the Kernel of Wheat from God and it was shocking to hear that He was going to die. He was so precious to them – how could His life end in such a meaningless way?

Jesus explained: "God has something better in mind: a plentiful harvest. If I die for the sins of humanity and am resurrected, then God will have a crop of countless people who can share in His life. I'm one now, but when I die I will live in millions of people all over the world." God did revive the Kernel of Wheat, raising Him up to give hope to all people.

Disciples are remarkable, not only because they follow Jesus, but also because Jesus lives in them. It's Jesus Immanuel – God with us – who gives strength to every believer.

# THE PRINCIPLE OF THE KINGDOM

*"… But if it dies, it produces many seeds."*
John 12:24

▶ This Scripture verse doesn't only describe Jesus' mission, but also the principle of the kingdom of God for every believer. Just as scared and reluctant as the disciples were because of Jesus' imminent death, we are also sometimes scared, and reluctant to let go of our own plans and interests. But if the kernel of wheat doesn't die, it can't yield a crop.

God's plans and interests are far greater than our own. Paul says it exceeds anything we can understand (see Phil. 4:7 and Rom. 11:33-36).

To give up your own plans and interests so that God's plans can grow and yield a plentiful crop is the great secret to the kingdom of God, bringing joy and happiness.

We might be sad when we have to let go of our dreams, but when God's plans grow from it, it is glorious. Allow the kernel of wheat to die in order to produce a plentiful harvest.

# NOVEMBER

# WHAT HAVE YOU DONE WITH JESUS?

*"He will prove the world to be in the wrong about sin and righteousness and judgment: about sin, because people do not believe in Me."*
John 16:8-9

There is a difference between "sins" and "to sin." The former is the result of the latter. Does that sound odd? Sins are all those things that we read about in newspapers and see on TV. However, to sin is to reject Jesus and not stand under His authority. All evil flows from it.

The Holy Spirit will not only convict the world of sin, but also that they have rejected Jesus and don't stand under His rule.

If people were to stand under His authority, there wouldn't be such sin in the world. The final judgment of God over people concerns just one question: "What have you done with Jesus?"

In every area of life where you don't submit to Jesus, the consequences of sin is evident. The Holy Spirit will be with you to help you follow in Jesus' footsteps. Don't ignore Him.

# IMPORTANT TRUTHS

*"I am going to the Father, where you can see Me no longer."*
John 16:10

This verse contains important truths. Firstly, Jesus would be going back to the Father. He is the High Priest of believers and the Judge of the earth. Even though believers would not see Him like they saw Him on earth, He would be with them in a new way. He would live and work in them.

Secondly, as Judge and Ruler of the earth, Jesus will judge all people according to their relationship with Him. Those who reject Him will be condemned, but those who accept Him will be with Him in great glory. Through His resurrection, Jesus was confirmed as the Truth of God. He is who He said He is, and is able to do what He said He would do.

Jesus' claims are not empty. The righteousness of God is on His side. He has the final say and the Father mightily confirms this truth.

# FRIENDSHIP WITH THE JUDGE

*For in the gospel the righteousness of God is revealed – a righteousness that is by faith from first to last, just as it is written: "The righteous will live by faith."*

Romans 1:17

The word "righteousness" explains an important concept: The fact that Jesus returned to His Father makes salvation a reality for all who believe in Him. He is the way to forgiveness and being made right with God.

Believers are not only forgiven, but made right with God. They can stand before Him clean and sanctified to love and serve Him. The Judge has not only acquitted the guilty parties, but He develops a close friendship with all His children. They can also be close to the Father's heart, just like Jesus.

The purpose of forgiveness is to restore relationships. God cannot have a relationship with sin; therefore the blood of Jesus forgave, saved and cleansed us so that we could have a relationship with God.

# WHERE DO YOU STAND?

*"The prince of this world now stands condemned."*
John 16:11

Believers know the final judgment over the whole earth is coming, but some parts of the judgment are already known: Satan has already been condemned by Jesus' blood on the cross. The devil's absolute rebellion and aversion of God have been exposed and condemned. His end is known, but with it also those who side with him.

Although the official verdict is yet to happen, the conviction and sentence has been written and finalized. The question to us is this: On which side of the bench do you want to stand? With the Judge or before the Judge? That's the message of the gospel.

It doesn't help to waste time over arguments about God's righteousness to condemn people who are not committed to Him. The important question is: "Where do you stand?" With God or against Him?

# JESUS DOES THE REST

*"I will make them come and fall down at your feet and acknowledge that I have loved you."*
Revelation 3:9

► Jesus' words to a small, weak congregation in the former town of Philadelphia had great power. These people were persecuted and slandered because they were committed to Jesus. But despite their hardships, they remained faithful.

"I will make …" Jesus says. He is actively involved in the situation. He is the Righteous Judge who has the final say and will see to it that people acknowledge the sincerity of the disciples' commitment to Jesus.

Moreover, the wicked will be forced to acknowledge that Jesus' love and blessing are on His followers. Jesus didn't just save the little church from their sufferings, but gave them victory and glory in the midst of it.

It is when we try to force people to recognize our testimonies that things can go terribly wrong. Focus on staying faithful to Jesus and He will do the rest!

# THE BIGGER PICTURE

*"My prayer is not that You take them out of the world but that You protect them from the evil one."*
John 17:15

▶ This is a strange prayer, isn't it? Jesus knows His disciples are going to suffer. So why doesn't He deliver them from suffering? Would that not have been better? The answer is because of love. How so? Jesus knew His disciples would live, even though they might die.

The disciples' testimonies to the world are the only hope for those who are unsaved. For the salvation of the world, Jesus carried the cross, and for the same reason His disciples endure their suffering. That's love – and greater love no one can find.

What is best for us is not necessarily what we think is best. When we suffer, we are likely to seek immediate deliverance, but God sees the bigger picture. It's important to trust God at times like this.

# GOD'S PROTECTION

*"My prayer is not that You take them out of the world but that You protect them from the evil one."*
John 17:15

Jesus' prayer doesn't ask for believers to be taken out of the world, but for them to be protected from the devil. They will need it, since the evil one plots against them. He will try everything to discredit their testimonies and faith, because his tactics are creative, sly and never ending.

God's protection will be there as long as believers stay close to Him. Nothing can snatch them from His hand. That's further proof to the world that God's word is true. The lives of believers will bear witness to this, including God's actions toward them.

Allow yourself to rest in God's hands. Even if your story doesn't end the way you'd like it to, it will always end in victory – God guarantees it. In God's hands, evil will never triumph.

# CHARACTER DEVELOPMENT

*"My prayer is not that You take them out of the world but that You protect them from the evil one."*
John 17:15

▶ Another reason why Jesus didn't pray for believers to be taken from the world was for their own good. God's glory is increasingly revealed in their lives through their spiritual growth and character development.

The saying "God is not interested in your comfort; He is interested in your character" is indeed true. Through obedience and faithfulness, believers experience the privilege of Jesus' spirit taking shape in their lives. As they get to know more of Him in every situation, so God is revealed in their lives more and more.

That's one of the most powerful victories over the evil one and his works. Character is not shaped when things go smoothly, but during the fiery furnace of life when we need to remain faithful to God.

Father, I often want to be taken from this world when things get too hard for me. Today I want to pray: Do what You want in my life, as long as I'm safely in Your hands. Amen.

# THE FAMILIAR
# IS STRANGE

*"They are not of the world,
even as I am not of it."*
John 17:16

These words make me think that a book should be written on this subject, entitled *The Strangeness of Jesus*. Maybe it has been written already! For believers, this peculiarity can sometimes come as a shock.

Believers are of this world – it's what they know and what's familiar to them. But with Jesus' Spirit in them, things change. Sometimes the world's arguments and ways of doing things are still the most logical and normal, yet there is something in them that disapproves.

Previously, Jesus' manner of doing things was strange, but the more we get to know Him, the more familiar we become with His ways. We call this process spiritual growth.

When Jesus' "strangeness" becomes your safe and familiar environment and way of life, then you know that you belong to God. His Spirit stands in contrast to the spirit of the world.

# THE WAY TO SANCTIFICATION

*"You have heard that it was said, 'You shall not commit adultery.' But I tell you that anyone who looks at a woman lustfully has already committed adultery with her in his heart."*
Matthew 5:27-28

One can, through one's own limited knowledge of God and His Word, easily fall into a trap of false security, self-righteousness and hypocrisy. Jesus is the complete revelation of God's holiness, far greater than the Ten Commandments.

Jesus proves that holiness is a state of the heart, and that apparent sincerity is no indication of true purity. A person who has never committed adultery is quick to think they are obedient to God in this matter, but Jesus points to what happens in the heart. What goes on in a person's heart is the real state of affairs. God is a God of the heart and His holiness is much greater that a list of do's and don'ts.

True holiness and sanctification before God is a deep, cleansing process that can only happen through the blood of Jesus. Religion on its own is woefully inadequate. To be cleansed by Jesus and to have a relationship with God is the only way to true sanctification.

# THE ONLY BEACON

*"Sanctify them by the truth;*
*Your word is truth."*
John 17:17

▶ What is truth? God's words are truth. Recently I visited dear friends who were going through a difficult time. "How should we handle this?" they wanted to know. I reflected on Jesus' life: "You have two choices: the way you usually do things, or God's way."

Choose the truth of God in the matter. Be dedicated to His truth, even when you're not used to it. Ask God what His truth is in your situation and allow Him to speak life into your situation.

Pull your crisis closer and grow in obedience to God through it. The truth of God is the only beacon for believers, not our emotions or instincts.

Each time a crisis or problem presents itself, you can choose God's truth or to do things your own way. Your choices become habits, and habits become character, therefore choose carefully.

# THE BEST INVESTMENT

*"Truly I tell you," Jesus replied, "no one who has left home or brothers or sisters or mother or father or children or fields for Me and the gospel will fail to receive a hundred times as much in this present age: homes, brothers, sisters, mothers, children and fields – along with persecutions – and in the age to come eternal life."*
Mark 10:29-30

Did you read correctly? Believers' inheritance is a hundred times as much as the family and property they've given up, plus the persecution they may have to endure? Yes, that's exactly what Jesus says.

Whatever you lose as a result of your relationship with Him, you will receive back a hundredfold in the family of God. All over the world you'll meet family members in Christ, where there'll be an immediate connection. Their homes will open to you, and they'll share what they have with you, just like you share with other believers. To be persecuted is normal to followers of Jesus, but their prospect is eternal life. There is no better investment than this!

Jesus' gospel doesn't promise a problem-free life. There will be many troubles and even prosecution because of Jesus, but God's promises surpass everything else.

# THAT WHICH REMAINS

*"Heaven and earth will pass away,*
*but My words will never pass away."*
Mark 13:31

The more we learn of Jesus, the more we get to know the Father. The more we learn of the Father, the better we can see things in perspective. The things that seemed so steadfast and long-lasting are suddenly insignificant. Indeed, this life is mainly "smoke and mirrors."

There is an end to it all, and what will remain? Everything that Jesus talked about! He is eternal and so are His words. May whatever you hold on to not be a handful of feathers, but eternal treasures from God. Hang them around your neck; write them on the tablets of your heart; arm yourself with them. In this way, your thoughts, words and deeds will stand firm when everything around you crumbles.

Lord Jesus, I don't just want to hear what You're saying – I want to live it! May Your words richly dwell in me, and may my words and deeds be deeply rooted in Your name. Amen.

# A LIFE WORTH LIVING

*"Truly I tell you, wherever the gospel is preached throughout the world, what she has done will also be told, in memory of her."*
Mark 14:9

Every person desires to leave a legacy that will say to those who remain behind: "My life was not wasted; it was worth it." People try to get this right in all kinds of ways. Others just give up and wither away in oblivion.

Jesus shows the best way to an eternal, steadfast legacy: to honor Him in the best way. Mary's bold, complete and self-sacrificing service to Jesus stands through all the ages as a beacon of love and worship.

She was an ordinary woman with an unimpressive life, but her love for Jesus stands eternal. It's like a monument that will stand even long after the world as we know it has disappeared.

As this life is speeding towards its end, you might wonder if it's all worth it. Know this: Everything will pass away, except your love and dedication to Jesus. That's what makes life worth living.

# REND YOUR HEART, NOT YOUR GARMENTS

*"I am," said Jesus. "And you will see the Son of Man sitting at the right hand of the Mighty One and coming on the clouds of heaven."*
Mark 14:62

When Jesus came before the council to be tried, the high priest asked Him directly, "Are You the Messiah, the Son of the Blessed One?" (Mark 14:61). Jesus' answer was just as straightforward: "I am." Then He added, "And you will see the Son of Man sitting at the right hand of the Mighty One and coming on the clouds of heaven."

Then the high priest tore his clothes – not as a sign of his conversion or reverence, but to show his horror and resentment of Jesus' confession. His contempt for Jesus and His words stood as clear evidence against the priest at Jesus' resurrection when the curtain in the temple tore in two. God said this through Joel: "Rend your heart and not your garments. Return to the Lord your God" (Joel 2:13).

Side with Jesus. He may be dismissed by the world, but He is the King of the nations. When He is revealed in glory, those who reject Him will be shamed.

# GRAB HOLD OF JESUS

*"Whoever believes and is baptized will be saved, but whoever does not believe will be condemned."*
Mark 16:16

▶ Although being baptized doesn't save you, it's the testimony of your salvation without which you will stand under God's wrath. God's judgment is for all people who don't take hold of Jesus through faith in Him. However, everyone who has taken hold of Jesus is completely exempt from God's judgment.

Not only can we rejoice because we were saved from the snares of sin, but we are also saved from being condemned for our sins. Sin brings judgment, and judgment brings death. Nevertheless, being baptized without believing in Christ is worthless.

Without faith you will face judgment – whether you are baptized or not. Whoever believes and testifies about their faith will be saved.

There is only one way to be freed from sin and be part of God and that is by grabbing hold of Jesus as the Shepherd of your soul. Without Him, any testimony is worthless.

# A GODLY DIET

*"It is written: 'Man shall not live on bread alone, but on every word that comes from the mouth of God.'"*
Matthew 4:4

Dieticians would agree that Jesus didn't have a diet in mind here, although one can easily be overwhelmed by the importance and necessity of everyday sustenance. It can easily become our all-surpassing driving force and concern. However, there is more to life than what we eat, where we live and what we wear.

We need truth to live, to build relationships, to work through hurt, to grow, to make contributions, to raise children and to grow old with dignity.

Achieving this can only be done with God's help. Without it we will be defeated. We live by every word that comes from the mouth of God ... not "most" or "more or less."

Make one of your life's questions, "What does God say about this?" and apply it to every situation you face. It's the answer that will save your life and keep you on the right path.

# "I WILL SPIT YOU OUT"

*"Because you are lukewarm – neither hot nor cold – I am about to spit you out of My mouth."*
Revelation 3:16

"I am about to spit you out" – these are strong words and only appear once in the New Testament. It actually means to vomit. Why would Jesus use such strong words? The answer is that someone who tries to serve two masters will not only frustrate both, but will gradually incur the contempt of both.

In the times in which we live we don't know how to deal with a Jesus who displays a righteous anger. We've processed Him as an all-accommodating Jesus who accepts everything and who always understands.

Theologians who have tried to shape Jesus into a generally accepted figure are stunned by a Jesus who is vomiting. This is because a Jesus who spits out lukewarm people makes us feel a little uncomfortable.

Jesus ministers to "cold" people so that they can become "warm," but "lukewarm" people want God's blessings while they're enjoying the sins of the world. He will reject them.

# LULLED TO SLEEP

*"Remember, therefore, what you have received and heard; hold it fast, and repent. But if you do not wake up, I will come like a thief, and you will not know at what time I will come to you."*

Revelation 3:3

Jesus' words to the church in Sardis were serious and harsh. The people there were exchanging the authenticity of the gospel and their precious commitment to Jesus for the philosophy and thought patterns of the day.

Jesus warned them that if they exchanged their lives for death, they risked being judged by Him. By moving away from Jesus and His message, they would subject themselves to the righteous judgment of the Judge.

The dilemma of Sardis is the same dilemma we face today: Many believers are influenced to follow the ways of the world, to their own detriment. In this way, the world is lulling the church to sleep.

Jesus' warning to be careful and not to be deceived comes to our attention once again. Don't adhere to things because they're popular. Depend only on the truth of Christ.

# FRIEND OR FOE?

*"Blessed are you when people hate you, when they exclude you and insult you and reject your name as evil, because of the Son of Man."*
Luke 6:22

A commitment to the Son of God brings the blessings of God. When the world hates us because of Christ, it means that our commitment is real, because the world doesn't abhor its own.

The treatment that the disciples can expect from the world is hate, rejection, name-calling and evasion. For many, it also means suffering and death.

For Christ's sake, they receive the curse of the world so that they can inherit God's blessings. Those who try to enjoy the best of both worlds will not be recognized by anyone – neither by the world, nor by God. Choose what you want to receive and from whom – a blessing or a curse.

Be careful what you choose, because that's what you'll get. Friendship with the world brings hostility with God, and friendship with God leads to hostility from the world. You will be blessed if you choose wisely.

# A POISONOUS ROOT

*"Woe to you who are rich, for you have already received your comfort."*
Luke 6:24

The biggest reason for the woes of wealthy people is not because they have a lot of money, but because they think it is their safe haven. It's easy for the rich to think that their financial means elevate them above ordinary people, and that wealth grants them a God-like status since they can make almost anything happen with their money.

That is where their misery originates: Their wealth creates an illusion that they don't need God, and then death swallows them.

Their joy is not in God, but in the privileges they are able to buy. Without God they have no future and no prospect of life and salvation.

About this issue, Paul writes: "For the love of money is the root of all kinds of evil. Some people, eager for money, have wandered from the faith and pierced themselves with many griefs" (1 Tim. 6:10).

# ANCHOR YOURSELF IN THE LORD

*"Woe to you who are well fed now, for you will go hungry. Woe to you who laugh now, for you will mourn and weep."*
Luke 6:25

The hunger and grief that people experience without God surpasses all that a person might face as a result of inadequate material resources.

There is nothing wrong with having enough to eat and enjoying life. However, those who enjoy abundance and laughter now, and think that's the sum total of life, will be rudely awakened.

Their sun will suddenly set while it's still day, and then no amount of fun or treats will bring any comfort. One often sees this happen: Marriages fail, children drift away from their parents, and people sink into despair and depression until they have no life left.

Don't seek consolation in anything other than the Person, character and ministry of Jesus. Enjoy your food and be thankful for it, but anchor yourself in the Lord to provide comfort for the soul.

# OUR ONLY TEACHER

*"The student is not above the teacher, but everyone who is fully trained will be like their teacher."*
Luke 6:40

Jesus' words are quite logical, but when you apply them to your relationship with Him they are also powerful. Jesus is our Teacher and we are His students. He teaches us to be like Him. We are not the teacher; He is. We don't do what we want or what we think is right; we do what the Teacher says.

We also don't do what other teachers (such as our culture or other people) say, but, like Jesus, we do only as the Teacher says. When we've heard and learned everything, we will be more like Him.

Paul wrote, "We will grow to become in every respect the mature body of Him who is the head, that is, Christ … attaining to the whole measure of the fullness of Christ" (Eph. 4:15, 13).

Don't let your life be dictated by anything other than what Jesus teaches. No form of patriotism, formalism or other loyalty can replace Him.

# TWO MISSIONS – ONE CHARACTER

*"As You sent Me into the world, I have sent them into the world."*
John 17:18

"As You sent Me, I have sent them." Isn't that awesome! The Father sent His Son into the world to witness about Him and to lay down His life for the reconciliation and restoration of everyone who believes in Him.

In the same way, Jesus sends us into the world to witness about Him and to lay down our lives for the restoration and reconciliation of everyone who believes in Him.

Paul says, "Even if I am being poured out like a drink offering on the sacrifice and service coming from your faith, I am glad and rejoice with all of you" (Phil. 2:17). We've received a godly mandate and an eternal example of how we are supposed to live out our testimony: Jesus Christ. As the Father treated Jesus, so Jesus treats us.

There is nothing more satisfying and fulfilling than living out your calling in Christ. This brings true meaning to life, and profound opportunities to the people around you.

# YOU ARE
# THE REASON

*"For them I sanctify Myself, that
they too may be truly sanctified."*
John 17:19

You are the reason why Jesus consecrated Himself to God to be crucified. He did it so that you could be devoted to God in the same way.

The phrase "truly sanctified" signifies the dedication and consecration that Jesus is talking about. Some people are dedicated to God, but driven by nationalism and culture. Some are motivated by the hope of prosperity and blessing; others by fear and distress.

Dedication that is driven by these things is superficial and short-lived. Dedication to God that is driven by truth will withstand all storms and temptations. For that exact reason Jesus died, so that you and I could be anchored in God for eternity, no matter what. Jesus' complete offering is for our complete ministry – unwavering and eternal.

Lord Jesus, I have a deep need to be anchored in the Father – to be dedicated to Him regardless of my circumstances. Minister to me, Lord, for this purpose. Amen.

# TIRED OF THE RUSH

*"I will not impose any other burden on you, except to hold on to what you have until I come."*
Revelation 2:24-25

The church in Thyatira was struggling (see Rev. 2:18-29). They were threatened by persecution from outside, and deception from inside. In the midst of the chaos, Jesus worked gently with them. He didn't ask anything extra from them, except that they hold tightly to Him.

Sometimes inexperienced leaders can burden a congregation if their approach differs from that of Jesus. Church members become tired of rushing after gifts and ministries and programs and goals. In the process they lose the gentleness and serenity of Jesus' ministry.

Zeal without wisdom is harmful and immature, which does not lead anyone to God's "green pastures" and "quiet waters."

A congregation that is tired of rushing after new fads has a need for the shepherding of Christ. Jesus says, "I will ask nothing more of you except that you hold tightly to Me."

# ALWAYS BE FAITHFUL

*"Be faithful, even to the point of death, and I will give you life as your victor's crown."*
Revelation 2:10

Being faithful is easy when things are going well, but faithfulness in the face of suffering requires special character and dedication.

Jesus says, "True faithfulness is to remain dedicated to Me even when there is no way out. Don't let your faithfulness be conditional – dependent on blessings and protection. Be unconditionally faithful so that you can inherit God's eternal life.

"There is more to God's life than your experiences on this side of eternal life. God's faithfulness goes beyond the grave! This life will pass away, but God's life is for all eternity." A good start is important, but Jesus wants us to remain faithful until the end.

To fiercely cling to this life makes us as miserable as the world. Our hope and faith must be separated from our circumstances. It should dwell in the Person and character of Jesus Christ.

# IT'S THAT SIMPLE

*"Yet I hold this against you: You have forsaken the love you had at first."*
Revelation 2:4

Much has been said about these words of Jesus, and still a lot remains to be discovered. The church in Ephesus was known for its spiritual maturity and work in spreading the gospel, but as the years passed, their focus weakened.

The main focus of the church was not to love Jesus and to serve Him with passion. He was no longer the main theme on the agenda. The same thing happens in society today. Gradually this lack of focus leads to stagnation and a blurring of our purpose on earth. Sometimes churches try to fix this, instead of just returning to Jesus.

Retain the simplicity and power of undivided passion for Jesus. Keep the ambition to grow in Him in all things. Don't let popular fashions and programs tarnish your vision. It's not worth it!

# LIVING BY
# THE SPIRIT

*"Whoever has ears, let them hear
what the Spirit says to the churches."*
Revelation 2:17

To be sensitive to the voice of the Spirit is a privilege. We tend to see and hear things from our own perspective and situation, but to be able to distinguish what God sees and says is the difference between life and death.

The Book of Revelation reveals Jesus in a dramatic way to the disciples. He gave unparalleled insight into the world of God and it is this knowledge that makes followers sensitive and alert to the voice of God in a given situation.

Furthermore, the knowledge of God's message puts a special responsibility on the churches. To comply with it is the most important thing they can do.

Father, may I be truly sensitive to the prompting of the Holy Spirit. There are few things in this world that confuse me as much, but I want to be guided by Your Spirit and truth alone. Amen.

# "LEAD ME ALONG THE PATH OF EVERLASTING LIFE"

*"Therefore consider carefully how you listen. Whoever has will be given more; whoever does not have, even what they think they have will be taken from them."*
Luke 8:18

People listen to Jesus in two ways: The one is to listen to what He says and to turn away, thinking they know it all. The other way is to take His words to heart.

The "know-it-alls" think they know best, but they have nothing, because without Christ they have nothing. They will be stripped of everything and stand naked in their ignorance.

However, those who take Jesus' words to heart will grow in the revelation of God and knowledge of the truth.

Accordingly, Jesus gives us this warning: "Pay attention to how you listen." Your attitude and mindset towards Jesus determines your whole life.

Don't let your heart deceive you. Pray like David: "Search me, God, and know my heart; test me and know my anxious thoughts. See if there is any offensive way in me, and lead me in the way everlasting" (Ps. 139:23-24).

# DECEMBER

# TOUGH LOVE

*"Those whom I love
I rebuke and discipline.
So be earnest and repent."*
Revelation 3:19

▶ Most congregations that suffer persecution receive words of chastisement from Jesus. This might be because believers tend to grab hold of all sorts of things to escape their affliction. All these alleged escape routes are dangerous traps designed to rob believers of Jesus. To let them be would be utterly unwise and loveless on Jesus' part. Therefore He rebukes and punishes, but with great love and care.

The person who becomes angry because of Jesus' discipline quickly moves to their own demise! The seriousness of being converted also emphasizes the urgency to turn back to Jesus' love and truth. Love doesn't come to us only in the form of comfort, but through discipline as well.

When we are disciplined, it doesn't always seem like something to rejoice about, but rather something to cry about. "Later on, however, it produces a harvest of righteousness and peace for those who have been trained by it" (Heb. 12:11).

# AS STEADFAST AS A ROCK

*"Martha, Martha," the Lord answered, "you are worried and upset about many things, but few things are needed – or indeed only one. Mary has chosen what is better, and it will not be taken away from her."*
Luke 10:41-42

▶ This reminds me of the following words Jesus spoke: "Do not work for food that spoils, but for food that endures to eternal life, which the Son of Man will give you" (John 6:27), and also: "Man shall not live on bread alone, but on every word that comes from the mouth of God" (Matt. 4:4).

We have many concerns in life, but only one is really crucial – to know what God wants and to submit to it. Even if we have an abundance of money and provisions, we will still die, and we can take nothing with us. God's words provide us with life, in this world and in the next. This is something that can never be taken away.

Help me, Father, to choose the best part, like Mary. I often get worked up over small things and feel far away from You. May my heart remain steadfast in Your words! Amen.

# CHRIST'S SERVANTS

*"These are the words of Him who holds the seven stars in His right hand ..."*
Revelation 2:1

The seven stars are the seven ministers or messengers of the seven churches in Asia Minor. It is significant and precious that Jesus holds them in His right hand; this symbolizes authority and honor.

Jesus adores them but also reigns over them in a special way. They serve in and under Christ's authority and their ministry and authority are not their own.

Would they want to stand under their own rule and start their own ministries? In so doing, they would lose the authority of Christ, as well as the glory of Christ. Should leaders start doing things in their own authority, they will have to give an account to Christ.

How wonderful are the feet of those who serve others with the gospel of Jesus! On the other hand, there is significant damage when leaders become their own messengers. Let us remember that Jesus is the ultimate authority over all the churches.

# CHRIST'S CHURCH

*"… And walks among the seven golden lampstands."*
Revelation 2:1

As we've discussed, the seven golden lampstands are the seven churches in Asia Manor. They are lamps because they shine the light of God's presence in a dark world. They are gold because they were divinely established and are God's property.

They stand in the midst of the world, but Christ stands in their midst. He is not uninvolved or standing at a distance; He is present in His churches to work in and through them.

Jesus not only knows what is going on inside them, but also how the world reacts towards them. He knows the enemies who want to destroy the church, and He's ready to act against them. Jesus is truly the Head of the church!

To acknowledge the presence of God inside the church is to be sensitive to the ministry and working of the Holy Spirit within the church. Slowing down the work of the Holy Spirit is denying the rule of Christ over the church.

# NOTHING MORE THAN A CLUB

*"If you do not repent, I will come to you and remove your lampstand from its place."*
Revelation 2:5

What happens to a church when Jesus does such a thing? If Jesus removes a lampstand from a church, He withdraws His presence and that church is henceforth no longer a church of God.

They would gather together and sing and preach, but the presence and power of God among them would be missing.

Then they're nothing more than a club or any other secular organization. Paul describes it well: "… Having a form of godliness but denying its power. Have nothing to do with such people" (2 Tim. 3:5). When Jesus is not at the center, that church no longer has value.

There are secular churches and spiritual churches; congregations of the world and churches of God. There are those who stand under Christ's authority and those who don't; those who don't love Him exclusively and those who do.

# A FOOL'S FOLLY

*"But God said to him, 'You fool! This very night your life will be demanded from you. Then who will get what you have prepared for yourself?' This is how it will be with whoever stores up things for themselves but is not rich toward God."*
Luke 12:20-21

The folly of the fool was that he thought his material possessions (his degrees and diplomas, connections and acquaintances, etc.) would provide him with security and life.

Such a person chooses to rely on the world rather than on God. God's reaction reveals three things: God is the Righteous Judge over people; He knows exactly what goes on in the hearts and lives of His people; and He calls everyone to account.

It's one thing if the world sees you as a fool, but it's something else if God calls you one. People judge according to their own preferences, but God judges in truth.

Evaluate your life. Do you also put your trust in materialism? Change your life while you still can. This warning carries a generous measure of mercy and grace with it – God doesn't want to catch you off guard.

# THE BLESSINGS OF OBEDIENCE

*"Since you have kept My command to endure patiently, I will also keep you from the hour of trial."*
Revelation 3:10

Our greatest protection is not what we pray for. It is the protection that comes through being obedient. People often follow their own way, and when evil arrives, only then do they start praying earnestly for protection.

Jesus confirms that protection comes automatically to those who are obedient. The protection that Jesus is talking about is not to keep us away from evil and tribulation, but to help us stand firm when it comes. David understood this well when he wrote, "Even though I walk through the darkest valley, I will fear no evil, for You are with me; Your rod and Your staff, they comfort me" (Ps. 23:4). There is no substitute for obedience.

To be a disciple of Jesus doesn't mean religious practice. It's a lifestyle of devotion and dedication to the Lord of lords and King of kings. Practice this.

# LET GO AND LET GOD

*"Who of you by worrying can add a single hour to your life? Since you cannot do this very little thing, why do you worry about the rest?"*
Luke 12:25-26

Worry is one of our favorite pastimes. It's also one of the biggest causes of disease and illness. Jesus' words emphasize how pointless it is.

Worry never contributes to the solution to a problem – it only depletes people's emotional resources, draining their energy and mind.

The alternative to worry is to let Jesus be Jesus. It's when people doubt if He really is in control and capable of guiding our lives that worry manifests. When we see God for who He is, worry loses its power.

What worries you – your children, health, money, friends, something else? Let it go. Ask Jesus to open your eyes to see what He sees, and watch what happens.

# MY HEART'S TREASURE

*"Where your treasure is, there your heart will be also."*
Luke 12:34

Your heart lies in the things that are most important to you. My family really matters to me; therefore my heart is with them. Are they more important to me than God's love and truth? Are yours?

There are many important things in our lives, but the question is: What is most important? That's easy to determine. Where is your heart most involved? What things do you focus on?

Your answers might differ from what you'd like them to be, but those are the things God sees. Jesus advises us to thoroughly inspect our hearts so that we don't stand ashamed one day when all is revealed.

The love of God spares no false foundations in our lives. Love wants to build up, restore and heal, and firmly plants us on the eternal Rock! In God's light there is no darkness.

# THE END OF
# ALL ARGUMENTS

*"I am the Alpha and the Omega,"*
*says the Lord God, "who is, and*
*who was, and who is to come,*
*the Almighty."*
Revelation 1:8

In some circles it's popular nowadays to say that Jesus was a religious leader of His time, even a political figure. However, today's Scripture verse surpasses any watered-down or distorted view of Him.

Jesus is the Beginning and the End of everything, all that is seen and unseen. He is the Almighty One; there is none like Him.

There is nothing more sobering than finding oneself face to face with Jesus. There is also no greater testimony against someone trying to convince their children that they cannot meet Jesus and that He will not change them. What other arguments are we left with?

Jesus doesn't need to be defended. Just allow Jesus to be Himself. The conviction of Jesus' presence – the glorified Jesus – discounts all arguments against Him.

# A FEAST IN GOD'S TRADITION

*"Invite the poor, the crippled, the lame, the blind, and you will be blessed. Although they cannot repay you, you will be repaid at the resurrection of the righteous."*
Luke 14:13-14

Commands like this often take me by surprise. If one wants to have a feast in God's tradition, you won't do it just to have a good time. You will certainly not do it to be rewarded by the same people at a later stage or to gain favor.

You would have a feast to invite the outcasts, and to acknowledge them and to serve them through your hospitality and respect. That's exactly what God does! Someone with this attitude will have life, says Jesus. God will reward them and recognize the work they have done for Him. This is what will happen at the resurrection! God's ways are refreshingly different.

Your thoughts may run wild at the application of the words in today's Scripture. Ask Jesus to show you how you can fulfill God's work in your life. It's not a recipe, but is something that is motivated by the purity of God's Spirit in you.

# BAD BEHAVIOR

*"I tell you that in the same way there will be more rejoicing in heaven over one sinner who repents than over ninety-nine righteous persons who do not need to repent."*
Luke 15:7

The Pharisees were pompous about their good deeds and godly lifestyles and liked to look down on the so-called sinners and Gentiles. In today's Scripture verse, Jesus says, "God rejoices more over one lost sinner who repents and returns to Him than over ninety-nine Pharisees who live righteous lives."

We all need to repent and be converted, but the Pharisees thought they didn't need to because they lived strictly by the Law. Self-righteousness is self-deception and robs us of the joy and glory of God.

Remember, Jesus also said, "Truly I tell you, the tax collectors and the prostitutes are entering the kingdom of God ahead of you" (Matt. 21:31). Not only does self-righteousness rob us of an abundant life, but God and people despise this kind of behavior.

Self-righteousness is something that both God and people feel strongly about. Remember, "God opposes the proud but shows favor to the humble" (James 4:6).

# CELEBRATE AND BE GLAD

*"'My son,' the father said, 'you are always with me, and everything I have is yours. But we had to celebrate and be glad, because this brother of yours was dead and is alive again; he was lost and is found.'"*
Luke 15:31-32

The religious, self-righteous Jews were upset because Jesus did so much for the masses and the Gentiles. Through this parable Jesus says, "You have all God's promises through His covenant with Abraham, and you have God's temple, yet still your hearts are not with God. He rejoices over the people who repent and turn to Him, but you sit puffed up in the corner.

"You want special honor and recognition, but you are farther away from God than the sinners and heathens!" It is wrong to think that we deserve a special place before God based on culture, race, church denomination or status.

There is nothing more pleasing to God than a heart that turns to Him. It's so much greater than elegant religious performances and traditions.

# COME, LORD JESUS!

*He who testifies to these things
says, "Yes, I am coming soon."
Amen. Come, Lord Jesus.*
Revelation 22:20

While we wait in anticipation for Jesus to return, it is important to note that Jesus has already returned in many ways. The world has experienced Jesus as Judge before, when He assisted believers and destroyed world systems that rose up against the church to destroy it.

Between Jesus' First and Second Coming He has not been inactive or passive. He is alive, powerful and very active. To the church in Pergamum, Jesus said, "Repent therefore! Otherwise, I will soon come to you and will fight against them with the sword of My mouth" (Rev. 2:16).

It's these "in-between" acts of Christ that strongly reinforce His Second Coming. Even though we've waited for 2,000 years, we're still waiting in anticipation.

The apostle Peter wrote, "The Lord is not slow in keeping His promise, as some understand slowness. Instead He is patient with you, not wanting anyone to perish, but everyone to come to repentance" (2 Pet. 3:9).

# THE LAST WILL BE FIRST

*Jesus asked, "Were not all ten cleansed? Where are the other nine?"*
Luke 17:17

This story is about more than just being thankful – it's about worship. Jesus healed ten lepers, yet only one turned back to thank and worship Him. The nine others used Jesus for His gifts, but only one worshiped Him as Lord.

This one man received more than just healing that day – He also received salvation for his soul. This is still the tendency today. Examine your own heart – do you use Jesus or do you worship Him? Test yourself: Do you still serve and worship Him even if He doesn't do what you ask?

The one man who turned back in the story was a Samaritan – an outcast to the Jews. By worshiping Jesus and not just using Him, in God's eyes this man who was "last" became "first."

Father, I don't want to use Your Son. I want to worship Him with everything in me, even when I don't get what I want. Your Son is Lord and King, and He is worthy to be praised. Amen.

# FOCUS ON CHRIST

*"The coming of the kingdom of God is not something that can be observed, nor will people say, 'Here it is,' or 'There it is,' because the kingdom of God is in your midst."*
Luke 17:20-21

▶ What a privilege to be able to announce that God's kingdom has come! It's a privilege that belongs to Jesus. People who don't understand Jesus and don't want to stand under His rule want to claim this privilege for themselves. They derive great fulfillment and self-interest from important "spiritual" announcements about God's kingdom.

However, Jesus says we mustn't pay attention to their self-centered practices. He has said what needed to be said: "The kingdom of God is in your midst."

Take hold of God's rule. Submit to it and chase after it with everything you have. The time is now. Don't be concerned about visible signs – rather concern yourself with Christ.

All the important things have been said: Jesus said them. Stick to them – don't be concerned about other things. There is nothing of interest beyond Jesus. Don't let anyone fool you.

# CLEAN CLOTHES

*"Blessed are those who wash their robes, that they may have the right to the tree of life and may go through the gates into the city."*
Revelation 22:14

Jesus said that the only way to receive the life God gives and to share in the fellowship of believers is by being born again. Such people allow themselves to be cleansed by His blood to stand as new creations before God in glory.

They are the new nation of God, redeemed and called from every tribe and nation, people and language. They sing a new song: "You are worthy to take the scroll and to open its seals, because You were slain, and with Your blood You purchased for God persons from every tribe and language and people and nation" (Rev. 5:9). They are blessed for all eternity!

Lord Jesus, how wonderful it is to stand before You as pure, because You have cleansed me by Your blood! There is no comfort in impurity, only death. Your holiness gives me life. Amen.

# THE BIGGEST OBSTACLE

*"You still lack one thing. Sell every thing you have and give to the poor, and you will have treasure in heaven. Then come, follow Me."*
Luke 18:22

I call this the rich man's surprise. Although his heart was sincere and he searched for God's kingdom, there was one big obstacle in his life: His security and safe haven were his wealth, not God.

Jesus knew this. That's why He said, "There is still one thing you haven't done. Sell all your possessions and give the money to the poor, and you will have treasure in heaven."

From the man's reaction, one can see that Jesus was right: The man turned away, sad and disappointed. We don't know anything more about him, but just think what could've been, had he done what Jesus said!

What is the obstacle that prevents you from fully serving God? Write it down. Are you going to be a follower of the rich man, or of Jesus? Will your life story in five years' time be different from his?

# NOT PART OF GOD

*"Outside are the dogs, those who practice magic arts, the sexually immoral, the murderers, the idolaters and everyone who loves and practices falsehood."*
Revelation 22:15

The people who don't share in God's blessings are those who don't share in God's plan of salvation. They may belong to a church, but not to the Body of Christ. Their way of living exposes them and so does their love for falsehood.

They live in contradiction to the character and ministry of Christ. False teachers reject Christ's truth, fraudsters reject Christ's integrity, immoral people reject Christ's purity, murderers reject the value of those for whom Christ died, and idolaters reject the sovereignty of Christ.

No person who rejects Jesus in this way will share in God's promises. To reject Christ is to love falsehood.

Don't allow the arguments of the world into your heart. They are aimed at Jesus and try to influence people in rejecting Him.

# JESUS' HEART

*"How often I have longed to gather your children together, as a hen gathers her chicks under her wings, and you were not willing."*
Matthew 23:37

This is such a sad Scripture verse. Two attitudes are evident: Jesus' attitude is to cherish, to gather and to protect; while the world's attitude is to refuse and to resist.

Jesus' words are sincere and intimate. Like a hen protects her chicks, Jesus wants to gather up His children, but the world doesn't care.

Forgetting the world's reaction, concentrate for a moment on Jesus' attitude. Can you imagine how He feels about you right now? Don't allow Satan to fool you. What Jesus says is how He feels about you – every day and always.

If you believe that this is how Jesus feels about you, let your heart stand firm in what He said. Let His words encourage and comfort you. Don't resist Him; allow Him to do what He so longs to do for you.

# TEAMWORK

*"Thus the saying 'One sows and another reaps' is true. I sent you to reap what you have not worked for. Others have done the hard work, and you have reaped the benefits of their labor."*
John 4:37-38

One of the most wonderful experiences of being a follower of Jesus is God-orchestrated teamwork. It's big and stretches across countries, cultures and world governments. Like a large harvester with thousands of parts and gears, God drives the lives of His children in this big task.

You don't fully realize the immensity of it and how God uses you in it. You are an important part of the team. It doesn't matter how great your role is – you're important and God is the driver. That's the whole point: One part is not more important than another. The whole team is important, and God above all.

Thank You, Father, that I can share in something so great. Help me to see more so that I can enjoy my share more. You are a great and wonderful God. Amen.

# TRUE REFRESHMENT

*"I am the Bread of Life. Whoever comes to Me will never go hungry, and whoever believes in Me will never be thirsty."*
John 6:35

People try to quench their thirst and still their hunger in all sorts of ways. Alcohol, drugs, food, shopping, pornography, lust, money, sports and a million other things are what people use to be satisfied.

The more people eat and drink of these things, the hungrier they become. There is a spiritual hunger inside each person that can only be filled with the Bread of Life – Jesus Christ.

If we ingest the Bread of Life, our spiritual hunger will be satisfied forever. Everyone who believes in Jesus will no longer be spiritually thirsty. Jesus' life in us becomes a life-giving fountain, which also quenches others' thirst and stills their hunger.

Father, thank You for Your only begotten Son, who quenches our thirst and satisfies our hunger for eternal life. Amen.

# SUBMISSION SETS YOU FREE

*"Very truly I tell you, everyone who sins is a slave to sin."*
John 8:34

I assure you, these words are not just an opinion. Years later, Paul explained it like this: "Do not let sin reign in your mortal body so that you obey its evil desires.

"Do not offer any part of yourself to sin as an instrument of wickedness, but rather offer yourselves to God as those who have been brought from death to life; and offer every part of yourself to Him as an instrument of righteousness.

"For sin shall no longer be your master, because you are not under the law, but under grace" (Rom. 6:12-14).

To be subject to God's rule doesn't bring bondage over your life – it saves you from everything that enslaves. That's the big difference between being a slave to sin, and being obedient to God.

# THE GOOD SHEPHERD

*"I am the Good Shepherd. The Good Shepherd lays down His life for the sheep."*
John 10:11

▶ God the Father sent Jesus into the world to lay down His life for the sheep. That's how Jesus leads – He doesn't come as the mighty general with a powerful army and destroys and conquers cities and countries. He has a different way of doing things. The Good Shepherd cares for His sheep by surrendering Himself to danger. That's how He leads and guides them to green pastures and quiet waters.

Jesus lays down His life for everyone who believes in Him and accepts Him. Peter said, "For you know that it was not with perishable things such as silver or gold that you were redeemed from the empty way of life handed down to you from your ancestors, but with the precious blood of Christ, a lamb without blemish or defect" (1 Pet. 1:18-19).

Father, we pray that we would follow in Jesus' steps to be good shepherds who are willing to lay down our lives for our brothers and sisters. Amen.

# AMAZING GRACE!

*"If you really know Me, you will know My Father as well. From now on, you do know Him and have seen Him."*
John 14:7

When we are born again, the Father places us in Jesus Christ, because Jesus and the Father are one, and so we can also become part of the divine nature.

Peter writes, "Through these He has given us His very great and precious promises, having escaped the corruption in the world caused by evil desires" (2 Pet. 1:4).

In Jesus we receive everything in the Father – the divine nature and eternal life. To know the Father means to share in Him through His Son, Jesus Christ.

That's amazing grace! Jesus came from the bosom of the Father to take us there too. Through Jesus Christ we have access to all the wonders and glories of God.

Father, thank You for choosing to make us part of Yourself through Jesus. Thank You for transforming us daily into Your image so that we can model Jesus to other people. Amen.

# WHAT A FRIEND WE HAVE IN JESUS

*"You are My friends if you do what I command."*
John 15:14

There are only two types of people in the world: those who resist Him, and those who obey Him – those who are His friends, and those who are His enemies. All people throughout the world can be divided into one of these two groups. Jesus' whole mission to earth was to make friends with His enemies.

Those who accept Jesus' offer become His friends and confidants. Those who reject Him will receive the wages of an enemy of God.

Let us, then, while the offer still stands, work to become Jesus' friend and confidant. We might lose our earthly friendships, but we will gain the greatest friendship of our lives!

"What a friend we have in Jesus, all our sins and griefs to bear! What a privilege to carry everything to God in prayer! Oh, what peace we often forfeit, oh, what needless pain we bear, all because we do not carry everything to God in prayer!" (Joseph M. Scriven).

# JESUS PRAYS FOR YOU

*"My prayer is not for them alone.
I pray also for those who will believe
in Me through their message, that all of
them may be one, Father, just as You are
in Me and I am in You. May they also be in Us
so that the world may believe that you have sent Me."*
John 17:20-21

▶ I don't know where you stand in your relationship with God today, but I know that He is talking about you. Jesus discusses you with His Father. You might feel that He doesn't notice you, but the prayer in this verse is for you – even ages before you were born!

Jesus longs for your relationships to be filled with love and maturity. He desires that you regard your wealth and riches from the perspective of being part of the family of God. He thinks the best of you and wants the best for you because He loves you. In Jesus you are part of a family where you matter and where you are safe. That makes your life special enough to convince the world that Jesus is from God.

Do you have people praying for you – a parent, a friend, a family member? If so, great! If not, remember, Jesus prays for you.

# PUT YOUR WEAPON AWAY

*"Put your sword away!
Shall I not drink the cup
the Father has given Me?"*
John 18:11

"Put your sword back into its sheath, Peter!" Jesus said. "Do you think anything will happen to Me that is not the Father's will? I stand under His authority and will never move away from it. My Father is completely in control of this situation – your intervention is unnecessary.

"I understand that you love Me and want to protect and defend Me, but understand this, Peter: God loves Me even more. If I don't go along with God's plan, you will never experience the joy of knowing God and having His Spirit in you.

"What the Father gives is good, even if it seems terrifying. Trust Him, Peter, no matter what. Even if I die, it's not the end. God's life and love will triumph."

Father, I often forget that You love me more than anything. I often forget that Your eyes are always on me and that nothing will happen to me that will catch You off guard. Thank You for this. Amen.

# SUDDENLY EVERYTHING MAKES SENSE

*"Peace be with you!"*
John 20:26

All Jesus' teachings over three years suddenly, with a bang, made sense and became meaningful to the disciples. Their world was violently turned upside-down. The shock was great, but the fear even greater.

In the midst of all the chaos, Jesus says: "God's blessings are upon you! His Spirit is with you. He conquered death and there is nothing to be afraid of. I am with you!

Let your hearts be calm. People can't do anything to you. Through Me you'll triumph, even in death. You stand under God's rule – He's in control. Nothing will separate you from Him. Peace be with you!"

Remain under God's control. Stay in His Word and the peace that transcends all understanding will guard your hearts and minds until you stand before His throne and see Him face to face.

# WHY DO YOU BELIEVE?

*"Because you have seen Me, you have believed; blessed are those who have not seen and yet have believed."*
John 20:29

There are two ways to see Jesus. One is the physical manifestation of His presence – how wonderful it would be to experience this! However, the most permanent way to see Jesus is through the spiritual revelation of His majesty and power.

It's a deep conviction of the heart that Jesus is who He said He is and that He will fulfill His promises. Happy and blessed are those in whose hearts the light of Christ has risen and whose eyes are opened to see the glory of Jesus' majesty!

To see and experience Jesus with an unveiled face brings everlasting change – into the image of Jesus. What a privilege!

Father, may You open the eyes of my heart to see the glory of Jesus. May Your Spirit shape and transform me more and more into His image. Amen.

# UNTIL THE END OF THE AGE

*"And surely I am with you always, to the very end of the age."*
Matthew 28:20

There is no greater comfort than to know that our Lord Jesus is always with us, even to the end of the age. Through everything we endure and experience, this truth stands anchored in the Person and Being of God.

It's not just on the peaks of life when we experience God, but also in the valleys and shadows of death. Many times it is precisely in the valleys when we feel God's presence the strongest.

There is nothing on earth too great or too terrible for God's majesty. While we run this race of life, our eyes need to be fixed on Jesus, and not on what's going on around us.

May the grace of the Lord Jesus Christ and the love of God the Father and the fellowship of the Holy Spirit be with you until we see Him face to face. Peace be with you!